Advance praise...

"*Dear Heart, Come Home* is an act of pure poetic kindness on Joyce Rupp's part. In sharing personally, she helps us become more gentle with ourselves and others, and more intimate with God. It is unique — filled with warmth yet at the same time practical and challenging. Classic Rupp!"

— ROBERT J. WICKS, author of *Seeds of Sensitivity*

"How refreshing it is to read of the treasures awaiting us in the unvisited depths of the second half of life. Joyce Rupp avoids the pessimism so prevalent in the coping-with-midlife books and instead invites us into the exciting adventure of being alive and living our true selves — at last!"

— DOLORES CURRAN, author of *Traits of a Healthy Family*

"I admire Joyce Rupp's book enormously. Don't just read this book — work, walk, play, and pray it!"

— L. PATRICK CARROLL, S.J., co-author of
Chaos or Creation: Spirituality in Mid-Life

"A book of wisdom for our midlife journeys! With her usual warmth and poignant vulnerability, Joyce Rupp lures us into the deepening places of our lives. Sharing her own diverse pathways, she encourages us to trust the many paths that lead us home to our own true self."

— MACRINA WIEDERKEHR, author of *The Song of the Seed*

Dear Heart, Come Home

Listen. Someone breathes
the lost name

Then clearly, in the mossy stillness, sings
Dear heart,
come home.

— DIANA ROWAN

Dear Heart, Come Home

The Path of Midlife Spirituality

JOYCE RUPP

A Crossroad Book
The Crossroad Publishing Company
New York

The author and publisher wish to thank the following for the use of material previously published:

The quotation from Diana Rowan on p. 2 is reprinted by permission of the author.

The excerpt from *The Divine Milieu* by Pierre Teilhard de Chardin on p. 33 is copyright © 1957 by Editions du Seuil, Paris. English translation copyright © 1960 by Wm. Collins Sons & Co., London, and Harper & Row, Publishers, Inc., New York. Renewed © 1988 by Harper & Row Publishers, Inc. Reprinted by permission of HarperCollins Publishers, Inc.

The quotation from Rabindranath Tagore on p. 52 is reprinted with the permission of Simon & Schuster from *Gitanjali* by Rabindrantath Tagore (New York: Collier, 1971).

"Suffering" by Jessica Powers on p. 136 is from *Selected Poetry of Jessica Powers*, ed. Regina Siegfried and Robert Morneau, and is used by permission of Sheed & Ward, 115 E. Armour Blvd., Kansas City, MO 64141. To order, call (800)333-7373.

The selection from Emily Dickinson on p. 142 is from *Selected Poems and Letters of Emily Dickinson*, ed. Robert N. Linscott (Garden City, N.Y.: Doubleday Anchor, 1959), and is used with permission of the Estate of Robert N. Linscott.

The quotation from Mary Oliver on p. 157 is from "The Summer Day" from *House of Light*, copyright © 1990 by Mary Oliver, reprinted by permission of Beacon Press.

This printing: 2004

The Crossroad Publishing Company
16 Penn Plaza, 481 Eighth Avenue, New York, NY 10001

Copyright © 1996 by Joyce Rupp
Photos Copyright © by Don W. Mendenhall

Printed in the United States of America

Library of Congress Cataloging-in-Publication Data

Rupp, Joyce.
    Dear heart, come home : the path of midlife spirituality / Joyce Rupp.
      p. cm.
    Includes bibliographical references.
    ISBN 0-8245-1556-0 (pbk.)
    1. Middle aged women–Religious life. 2. Middle aged persons–Religious life. 3. Middle aged women–Psychology. 4. Middle aged persons–Psychology. 5. Spiritual life–Christianity. 6. Rupp, Joyce. I. Title.
BV4579.5.R87 1996
248.8'4–dc20
                                                    95-51419
                                                       CIP

For

Bernice Hill

and

Irene Sheiner Lazarus

two wise women
who helped immensely
while I searched
for home

Contents

Preface

the persistent voice of midlife
wooed and wailed, wept and whined,
nagged like an endless toothache,
seduced like an insistent lover,
promised a guide to protect me
as I turned intently toward my soul.

as I stood at the door of "Go Deeper"
I heard the ego's howl of resistance,
felt the shivers of my false security
but knew there could be no other way.
inward I traveled, down, down,
drawn further into the truth
than I ever intended to go.

as I moved far and deep and long
eerie things long lain hidden
jeered at me with shadowy voices,
while love I'd never envisioned
wrapped compassionate ribbons
'round my fearful, anxious heart.

further in I sank, to the depths,
past all my arrogance and confusion,
through all my questions and doubts,
beyond all I held to be fact.

finally I stood before a new door:
the Hall of Oneness and Freedom.
uncertain and wary, I slowly opened,
discovering a space of welcoming light.

I entered the sacred inner room
where everything sings of Mystery.
no longer could I deny or resist

the decay of clenching control
and the silent gasps of surrender.

there in that sacred place of my Self
Love of a lasting kind came forth,
embracing me like a long beloved one
come home for the first time.

much that I thought to be "me"
crept to the corners and died.
in its place a Being named Peace
slipped beside and softly spoke my name:
"Welcome home, True Self,
I've been waiting for you."

—JOYCE RUPP

MY MIDLIFE JOURNEY has taken me deeper than I ever dreamed I would go. It has not always been a journey that I have chosen. I have felt, at times, that I was being pushed and shoved forward on the road that would set me free. At other times, I relentlessly pursued the path that led down to the darkness where wisdom waited to greet me. Throughout much of this time I was unaware of the quiet yet persistent growth taking place within me.

I began keeping a personal journal when I was twenty-seven years old. I did so out of the loneliness and pain that were a part of my life then. (My younger brother had recently died, and I was working in an area that was far from loved ones.) As I began journaling, I quickly discovered that it was a way not only to keep in touch with my inner self but also to draw forth some of the mystery of my being and the well-kept God-secrets that dwelt there. I have made entries in my journals almost every day since that early decision to write. Over the years I have been amazed at the words that formed themselves on the pages. Tears have often come as I've reread the journals and felt a Power much greater than myself moving through those words.

About five years ago I realized that I wanted to share some of my inner journey during the midlife phase because that is when I grew the most and where I discovered profound wisdoms. It is the time when I most clearly heard the call to come home to my true Self.

I firmly believe that the deeper down we go the more it is possible to experience some common elements of the psyche, such as existential loneliness, yearnings for truth and meaning, fear of the darkness, and longings for inner peace. I am convinced that if I can be honest and vulnerable with my own process, others will draw courage and comfort from it because they will see some of their own life reflected in mine. This sharing is not easy for me to do. As an introvert I feel as if I am walking naked on the pages. But I also believe that I am called to do this and I want to honor this call from within.

When Susan Shaughnessy promotes the value of journal-keeping, she suggests that not only the process of writing but also a review of the content of journals at a later phase in one's life can be a good resource of growth. Shaughnessy writes: "And there they [the journals] lie, waiting until a time when you revisit them and sift for gold."[1] This was my endeavor as I walked through my midlife history.

It was both painful and joyful for me as I read my personal journals. I had to revisit some unwanted emotions and difficult situations that I preferred to avoid. I learned that my forty-third year was probably the key year of my midlife process. During that year I had major surgery; a very dear friend died of cancer and another one was diagnosed as terminally ill; my father died suddenly; my mother moved from the home she had known for forty-nine years, and the director of my workplace went through an emotional upheaval that affected all of us on staff.

While I read through this pain and other struggles previous to and following my forty-third year, I discovered how much I had grown from these difficulties. Although I felt healed from much of my midlife journey, more healing happened as I reviewed these journals. I marveled at the truths I had taken to heart and the resiliency of my spirit in moving through times of darkness and discouragement while retaining so much enthusiasm for life. I also saw, with sorrow, how harsh I was with myself in earlier years and read, with anguish, the relational struggles with others that I had experienced.

At times, there was a richness and a depth to my journal entries. I could see wisdom growing and maturity evolving in my spiritual life. I was also constantly astounded at how different I am today than I was at an earlier age. I am much more self-assured, open to life, accepting of others, and surrendered to God than I was in my early thirties. Hope and gratitude continually moved through my being as I did this work.

I also found countless images throughout my journal entries. As I rediscovered these images, I saw how each one had been a source of inspiration and encouragement. So often what gave me the strength to continue and not give up were the potent images that kept surfacing. They helped me to name my emotional states and gave me the courage I needed to go deeper to find meaning, especially during times of inner confusion and emptiness.

The images that are in my journals came during times of meditation, hiking, journaling, dreams, quiet contemplation of the earth, and at other ordinary moments of my life. The source of these images was mostly from deep within myself, but sometimes the images came from other sources such as novels, myths, songs and poems, spiritually and psychologically oriented books, and the Hebrew and Christian scriptures.

As I grew in my awareness of how powerful images had been for me, I longed to encourage others in their use of images, particularly during midlife. It is my hope that the themes and images that are offered to you in the following chapters will gift you with encouragement. May you discover and name your spiritual path through these images as well as through other images that are revealed to you. As you go deeper, may you gain greater clarity and a stronger sense of affirmation about your own resources, vitality, and goodness as a person of generativity. May you continue to discover and come home to your true Self.

Acknowledgments

WITH EACH BOOK I WRITE I become more aware of how I do not write alone. So many persons help to bring a book to life. This is especially true of *Dear Heart, Come Home*. I am particularly grateful to all those women and men who risked being vulnerable, who took the time to reflect on their midlife process through the Questionnaire and the Gatherings. My special thanks to those who organized these Midlife Gatherings for me.

This book first came to birth as a thesis that I wrote while I was a student of the External Program of the Institute of Transpersonal Psychology in Palo Alto, California. My work with the Institute was a powerful experience in personal growth and consequently gifted me with the opportunity to research and write about midlife.

Much of my time in research and writing was spent in the guest house of the Benedictine sisters at the Abbey of St. Walburga in Boulder, Colorado. I cannot say enough about the hospitality and goodness of this community. I also found solitude and beauty at Sharon Samek's mountain home, which she generously shared with me.

My readers of the manuscript were invaluable to me with their advice and insights: Carola Broderick, Dolores Curran, Kathy Cosgrove Green, William Fitzgerald, Marla Kaurez, Rita and Bob Mailander, Marie Micheletto, and Macrina Wiederkehr.

I gathered a Midlife Women's Group to "try out" the book. They read and studied each chapter and participated in the opening and closing rituals. What a wonderful group they were and how much laughter and tears we shared. Thank you Joyce Hutchison, Nicola Hiatt Mendenhall, Linda Chiesa Rudkin, Pat Ryan, and Marge Monaghan.

There are many others whose lives also touched mine and helped this manuscript to come to birth: Joelle Mauer, Thomas M. Zurek, Marge Cashman, Thomas J. Pfeffer, the Pat and Edna Carney family, Dorothy Sullivan and Janet Barnes who daily prayed for my work, my mother, Hilda Rupp, who not only birthed me but has blessed my life constantly with her wisdom and friendship, and my Servite community members who cheer me on.

My new association with Crossroad Publishing Company has been a joy. I greatly appreciate the vision and vitality of Michael Leach, publisher, and the expertise of editor John Eagleson, who was very careful with my manuscript. I am delighted with the work of Don W. Mendenhall, photographer, and count myself blessed to have his photos in this book.

There are many more whom I wish to thank, all those who remain unnamed or hidden behind the scenes: those who have been kind enough to write to me, those who have participated in my conferences and retreats and shared their life experiences with me.

My thanks to all of you. You are each a part of this book.

Introduction

*But human beings need deepening places, too. And far
too many never have any. Think about your deepening
places, Meg.*

— MADELEINE L'ENGLE

MIDLIFE IS MORE THAN A CRISIS. It is a summons to grow
and a challenge to change. Midlife beckons one inward.
It is a move to interiority, a passage to the deeper places
where we discover our authenticity, where we realize both our limitations and our grandeur. It is here that we come home to our
truest Self. We take our external experiences with us to the inside
and look at our life. We evaluate our goals, hopes, dreams, beliefs,
behaviors, experiences — all that has marked us and contributed to
the person we have become — and we ask ourselves: "Is this the
person I want to be in the future?"

Midlife doesn't go by a precise chronological timepiece that automatically tells us when it is time to evaluate our lives, although
most adults experience this stage of growth roughly between the
ages of thirty-five and sixty. I have learned that each person's
midlife journey is unique. While some midlife characteristics and
themes may fit each person, there are always exceptions and unique
experiences.

I recall a man who told me that he wasn't "a wealthy execu-
tive who'd retired early and left a wife in order to marry someone
younger." He felt that this was the typical portrait of men in midlife and that most authors focused on the external changes of life
instead of the internal ones. He was a struggling middle-class male
in his early fifties who had lost his job and didn't know what he
wanted in life. At the same time, he was much more focused on
the inner life than on the external pursuits of a new woman or a
new hobby, as many midlife men are described.

Similarly, while some midlife women may be experiencing the
"empty nest" syndrome, others may be like a woman in her early
forties who had two young children. She was enjoying this dimen-

sion of motherhood in her life and was just beginning to discover the thrill of the spiritual path unfolding for her. She felt that her children were helping her in this discovery and that she had experienced a lot of midlife issues in her thirties.

C. G. Jung recognized that what works for the adult person in the first half of life will not work for the second half. Each person's journey will unfold in a way that calls her or him to growth. Many books on midlife have been written since Jung first proposed that this period of adult growth is every bit as painful and unpredictable as the stage of adolescence. This stage is variously referred to by authors as "midlife," "middle age," "middle years," or "the middle passage."

Many people automatically refer to midlife as a "crisis." Webster's Dictionary defines "crisis" as "the turning point in the course of a disease when it becomes clear whether the patient will live or die." Midlife is a turning point, a time when one can no longer go by the dreams and the life-approach of one's youth. To simply continue the way one has from youth onward can mean death for one's ability to grow. Midlife is an opportunity to turn toward greater life or wholeness.

Webster's Dictionary also describes "crisis" as an intensely painful attack of a disease, a time of great danger or trouble. This traumatic, crucial time might also be a part of midlife, although not all adults experience it in this way. I, for one, have not had an extended time when I felt that I was in peril and in danger of completely falling apart. However, I have had times of ongoing intense struggle and spaces of life when I wondered if I would ever be happy again.

I personally prefer to speak of this stage of adult development as a journey, a movement toward a new, unknown destination. Midlife is a time during which things are shifting, moving, taking a different form or shape. The midlife journey is a gradual unfolding, a time of choices and decision-making, where the person we are choosing to be is eventually revealed to us. This coming home to our true Self is not something we can hurry or force to happen quickly.

In midlife, we look at who we've become. Insights, values, beliefs that we so eagerly sought and developed in our youth and carried around for years beg for our attention in dreams, irritations and frustrations, fantasies, and longings. Gradually, we sort out what we want to keep and what we need to leave behind. It is no easy task. All this "stuff" hangs onto us like barnacles. We feel undressed without these things. We think this is who we are, but we can no longer carry this clutter along with us. We must let go of guilt and shame, certain thoughts and behaviors, dreams that will never be lived in this lifetime, wounds that have created barriers to self-esteem or inner peace. Perhaps the toughest of all, we must come face to face with our mortality and acknowledge that this life as we have come to know it is passing away.

Not everyone accepts the challenges of going deeper that the midlife journey demands. Janice Brewi and Anne Brennan, authors of numerous books on midlife, recognize that an adult can close himself or herself off to this experience: "One can deny that a volcano is erupting and just freeze in one's place and become a petrified, hardened fossil. One can die at forty and not get buried until ninety."[1]

What Is Spirituality?

The midlife journey affects all of who we are, including our spiritual path. There was a time in my twenties and early thirties when spirituality was a separate compartment of my life. I always viewed it as larger than religion but it was a sacred space that was separate from the rest of life. I felt that my work and relationships took me away from God (my personal prayer, meditation, sacred ritual) instead of drawing me into God. I had a strong God-me approach. Although I was deeply searching and longing for the Beloved, I set very specific limits on where and how I could find and commune with this God.[2]

It was not until my late thirties that I understood and accepted the Merton-based theory of spirituality that recognizes the life of the whole person as being in relationship with God. This relationship is not static but dynamic, always involving a constant movement of transformation. Spirituality touches and influences every other part of my life and every other part of my life touches and influences it. My spiritual life is always in process. I never come to the point where I am "finished" with it. Spirituality is not a matter of doing things right so that I can get to a place of perfection and not have to grow anymore. Rather, I am always moving into new realms of transformation. It is an exciting venture filled with mystery, one that can provide a source of nourishment and meaning.

Spirituality has an ethical component to it. It influences who we are and how we are. Living authentically or ethically are vital aspects. Spirituality also has different connotations depending on our gender. Irene Claremont notes:

> [Women's spirituality] implies relationship in its very essence: relationship to God in those intangible fleeting moments when she is aware of a presence, whether it be in the sudden impact of a white cherry tree in blossom, or the rhythmical furrows of a ploughed field; whether it be in a moment of unforgettable union with another human being or alone in the stillness of her own silence. Wherever it may happen there is for her always relationship.[3]

Spirituality for men often implies more of an idea or a theory about how to live one's life. According to Patricia Hopkins and Sherry Ruth Anderson, men often place more emphasis on the ethical than on the relational aspect. These authors interviewed hundreds of women and discovered a key difference from men's spirituality in that women have not trusted their own experience. Women have looked to authority figures outside of themselves for this truth. Women are only now discovering the value of their intuition, the necessity for solitude (for which they have longed), and the need to trust what they experience as sacred in their lives, whether this be through relationships or nature or other meaningful sources.[4]

What About Images?

I believe that images can have a profound, positive effect on how one travels through this stage of adult growth. Images can help to name one's midlife experience and to stay more focused and centered while growing into the second half of one's life. Positive images can comfort and console, challenge and guide. They can be trusted companions during those seasons when the search for identity seems helplessly mired in the dregs of "blah-ness" and meaningless activity.

Images are often associated with the emotional dimension of an event or an experience. When I have difficulty trying to name my emotional state, I often pause to allow an image to float into my consciousness. How quickly I connect my inner and outer worlds. Some of the images that have arisen during times of midlife travail are:

> An off-key melody, a journey with no maps, falling into a dark tunnel, standing at the garden and yelling "grow!," an empty, waiting basket, a sharp knife slicing the air, getting my foot caught in a slamming door, a table full of unknown and untasted foods. (P. J. — Personal Journal)[5]

Images provide a rich resource for discovering the interior life. Mircea Eliade believed that if we are without images, we are cut off from our soul.[6] "It is here, in the inner landscape, where we can catch a glimpse of the Sacred. Symbol, myths, and images are treasures of the psyche and are the very substance of the spiritual life."[7]

Jean Dalby Clift, author of *Core Images of the Self,* describes an image as something concrete, having specific meaning, that helps us connect at some level with ourselves. She believes that each person has core images that are central to life and personality. These images affect one's life by acting as transformers, giving energy for healing. These core images are found in a variety of sources such as one's earliest memory, stories that one loved or hated as a child, dreams, and songs. By listening to the existence and the movement of these themes in our lives we can gain greater inner freedom and obtain new levels of meaning in life.

When Kathleen Fischer writes of faith and the imagination, she refers to a Hopi Indian myth in which the Cloud People travel on rainbows, bringing messages between heaven to earth. These Cloud People are the Sun and Earth's means of communicating with one another and with humankind. Fischer notes that "the imagination is our inner rainbow....It is the bridge which joins God and the earth, the sacred and the secular, bringing them into a unity in our life."[8] Images are like ships traveling between two worlds of ours, the conscious and the unconscious, the concrete and the intangible, carrying messages from one to another. Images can help to convey the meaning of our lives in areas that are difficult to name and comprehend.

What Have Others Experienced?

While I knew and trusted my own midlife experience of images, I felt a need to test this theory with the experience of other adults who were either currently in midlife, or just beyond it, to see if they, too, had the experience of images arising and if these images were helpful for their midlife process. Thus, I designed a Midlife Questionnaire to be given to individuals who then came to a follow-up meeting, a "Midlife Gathering," to discuss their responses.[9] I asked only seven questions of the respondents. The first two centered on what their understanding of spirituality and midlife was. The other questions focused on naming and describing their images, noting any significance that the images might have had for their spiritual growth.[10]

The most common and consistently repeated theme of the respondents was that of control — recognizing their limitations and letting go of the belief that, if they just worked hard enough or figured things out well enough, they could make life go the way they wanted it to go.

A few of the respondents expressed confusion or distress in trying to name images in their midlife journey. Yet, when images were shared by others in the groups, those who had expressed difficulty with the use of images quickly resonated with the images that were given. This happened at every Midlife Gathering. At the first gathering, one woman said she just didn't "think in images." Later on, another respondent shared her image of an African violet. She told us that when this plant was given to her, it was in full bloom. Eventually, it stopped blooming and became ragged-looking. Her friend told her that if she cut the plant down to its roots and placed it in a dark room for about thirty days it would put out fresh shoots and form new blooms. When she did this, the plant "came back to life" and was beautiful again.

This woman told us that she had cut the plant down three or four times, commenting: "Each time my life has gone through another cycle of 'pruning' it has been time for my little plant to be cut back and put in the dark. This plant speaks to me of faith and hope in the midst of transition and is a reminder to care for my own life." As this story was told, everyone in the room was shaking their head "yes" with understanding, including the woman who had said she did not "think in images."

When persons who do not naturally think in imagery are given symbols, they can often identify with them because the images provide a vehicle to another level of experience and response. I also noticed, at other times, how these persons used images without even realizing they were doing so (e.g., "My life is at a crossroads").

I was amazed by the enthusiastic response to the Midlife Questionnaire and the Midlife Gatherings and astounded at how open and vulnerable the respondents were. Each one took the deep parts of his or her life and shared them generously. It was humbling to experience this and also very gratifying. I felt a kinship with the respondents. They confirmed my own understanding of spirituality as well as the midlife themes that were so much a part of my life. They also verified my belief regarding the presence and the effectiveness of images for midlife spiritual growth. Thus, the chapters of this book contain material not only from my journals but also from the respondents. I begin each of the chapters with material from my own experience of midlife and follow it with a mixture of information from midlife literature and the respondents' questionnaires.

CHAPTER ONE

Midlife Interiority: Going Deeper

Each one of us must reach inside ourselves to find our own power sources.

—SANDRA INGERMAN

Deep
is where it is dark
where there is mystery
where the way is not known
where it is easy to become fearful
and even turn back.

but
Deep
within your heart,
God,
is where
there's always strength to go in
where truth becomes known
where your love holds me close
where I need not be afraid.

my hidden self,
Deep, Deep down
in the womb of Yourself:
safe
nourished
guarded
enlivened.

take me there, God.
I want to go.

—Joyce Rupp

O N THE COVER of one of my journals I placed a print of a woman standing in solitude by a large, open window. She faces outward, looking into a mysterious Monet-like woods. There is a numinous quality to her attentive presence. This mood speaks to me of the movement between the conscious and the unconscious, of connecting the outer world and the inner world. There is a sense of mystery and wonder. Whatever it is that the woman is observing, it is obviously reaching back into the depths of her soul. Something or Someone beckons to her and holds her there at the window.

I was attracted to that print because I felt that I had some of those same soul-reaching moments in my midlife growth. I believe that in midlife God calls to the soul: "Move beyond what you know. Now is the time to risk the hidden path of going deeper. Go into the stillness and solitude within you. Come, find your true Self." This is a call to become more grounded or rooted in our strengths and our wisdoms — those inner treasures that wait to be discovered as we enter unknown, inner territory and reflect upon our life.

I never planned to "go deeper," but the call to do so came very forcefully while I was in the desert, a most appropriate place to seek the deeper things of life. I was forty-one and had gone to the Desert House of Prayer to make an eight-day retreat. I went with an overwhelming tiredness from all the rush and run of life. I felt I could have slept for months. My bones hurt from overwork and my heart ached for solitude. I was out of sorts with myself and still hurting from a painful, final break with a mentor and trusted confidant of my spiritual journey, one whose life choices had left me disillusioned and heartbroken. In reality, I was struggling with many pieces of my life and this particular hurt was just one of them. At the same time, I felt a strong trust that God would provide opportunities for my healing. I believed I would receive some inner direction if I stopped running long enough to listen to this deeper part of myself.

I walked rather aimlessly among the wild desert plants and creatures on the first days of retreat, seeking refuge from my burn-out and from the still-deep pain within me. One day, midway through the retreat, I found myself sitting on a large boulder, confused and anxious about my relationship with God. Why did this relationship seem scattered and distant? Why did I feel so hollow and unnourished? I knew that I longed for greater intimacy and union with God yet I had tasted none of this for a long time. What was God asking of me? What more was needed? Had I failed in some way? Had I not done my part to urge greater communion? What was missing and how could I find it?

As I sat there, two words suddenly stood up in my soul as clear as Orion on a cloudless night. "Go DEEPER," they said. I listened for more. Nothing there. Only those same words with greater emphasis: "Go deeper. It is time." Tears gushed up as I felt the curtains of my inner life part and Fear come out to make a first of many appearances: "What does this mean? Can I do this? How will I do it? What will I find? How much will it hurt?" How ironic, I thought, that I who have longed for God and for the truth of myself would now be terrified of the invitation to head in that precise direction.

I sat on the boulder most of that day. I mulled over "go deeper." I ate my lunch. I argued with the voices of fear and anxiety. I wrote down my thoughts and feelings. I pondered. I grimaced at what I figured would be a lot of future pain. I cried. I thought back to my first day in the desert to the anxious fears I'd felt about getting lost as I hiked in unknown territory, of being bitten by snakes and scorpions, or being attacked by the wild pigs. By day three I was at home there and had almost none of those fears so I knew — at least in my head — that fear could be sent on its way.

Then I delved back into my memory and looked at how I had known God. I had often experienced this God as unconditionally loving, compassionate, and faithful, a constant source of inner strength and courage. I knew that I could trust this God with my journey.

The more I reflected on "go deeper," the more I understood this to mean "go deeper into the heart of God" which was mysteriously also the heart of myself.[1] I felt somewhat comforted by this. I also sensed that this was a call to *listen* ever more closely, which meant I'd have to be very quiet and attentive.

Finally, before the sun set in the low Arizona sky, I realized that this day was an immensely graced one. I asked God if I could do it, if I could really go deeper. It seemed that God said: "If you want to, you can." It was then that I stood on the hillside in the desert and praised God who had visited me, who had revealed the call to go more deeply into the divine heart by going more deeply into my own. I stood there and I proclaimed:

> On this desert hillside in Arizona, I hereby pledge my love to you again, God of my life. I accept the invitation to go more deeply into your heart. I consider it a wonderful honor, responsibility, and challenge. I know you will give me what I need in order to do this. (P.J.)

All of this may sound dramatic but it didn't feel that way then, and it still doesn't.[2] The call to go deeper was very real on that day, however. It was a turning point for me, offering me something that I had longed for but was unable to name: a new way to be with God and a coming home to my truest Self. I had received a desperately needed hope for my midlife journey.

I left the retreat but the words did not leave me. They pursued me back into my work and invaded the territory of my life. During the next three or four weeks after the retreat those two words, "go deeper," kept surging into my consciousness. I gradually felt more secure and less fearful about the call, although fear, doubts, and questions returned at various times to hound me. I lost sight of this call many times in the coming years, but I kept coming back to it, or rather, it kept coming back to me. When I tried to run from going deeper, my dreams would catch me, or a circumstance of life would demand that I return to the depths.

God held me to my pledge and gave me golden discoveries that I never could have anticipated. At times, these discoveries were tensed with pain and turmoil; at other times, they were riddled with mystery and confusion. Yet again, they were giant sighs of relief and welcomed bits of truth.

Throughout the journey of going deeper, constant images arose to encourage, challenge, and confirm my process. I had never enjoyed rainy days. I was a "sunshine person." Surprisingly, I began to feel at home with rain, sensing a certain stillness inside of me on cloudy, moist days. Rain gradually became an image of comfort, a companion to the silence within. I made many journal entries about rain. One spring day I wrote:

> late March rain
> threatens to soon be snow.
> all through the dark night
> it made its mark on earth.
> I look out my window
> and the concrete walls
> are wet with the falling.
> they patter away on the rooftop
> like an old friend calling home.
> I pause to say hello
> and feel welcome in my heart.
> come again, I say to the rain,
> you gentle me and lift me up,
> or is it rather, you send me down,
> down to the stillness inside,
> down to where I need to be ... (P. J.)

Another image that took on great significance for me was that of the moon. I had always focused on the sun with its energy and vitality. The reflective stillness of moonlight did not draw me until I heard the midlife call to go deeper. Over and over I experienced the moon as a comforting presence that wooed me and watched over me. I relished night walks in the subdued light of the full moon. I felt a pull from the moon that was directly related to the pull I was sensing from God:

> I am held captured
> by a Power far beyond me.
> up and up it rises
> like a full moon in October.

I cannot turn away.
It holds me in its glow
and energizes me
in a compelling sort of way.

Words I know not what
surge through my being,
demanding an entrance
into the domain of my life.

It is you, God, this I know.
You are the Power surging.
You are the Compelling Presence.
It is you who hold me in attention.

I am lost in the aura.
I am taken to the Deep.
It matters not what the meaning,
only the truth of the meeting.
You have arisen in my heart,
I have been drawn into Love.
It is profoundly draining.
It is magnificently sacred. (P.J.)

Sometimes the images that spoke to the call to go deeper were
harsh ones that challenged me and led me to feel the pain of the
interior process. Oftentimes when I entered the deepening places
of myself I experienced a wordless unknown that took a long time
to be named. I couldn't tell what was happening inside. I only knew
that I felt restless, sad, and unsettled:

what is it in me?
all this long week
the unnamed ache
the almost tears
the unbloody wound
the hollow space

what is it in me?
something is crying out
to be heard
to be felt

unfinished business?
just the early 40's rising up?
I wonder.

I do not want to deny
I do not want to ignore
I want to be free
I want to be who I am

should I go deep?
must I look long?
I wonder
I wonder (P.J.)

The image of roots also spoke to me but in a much different way. This image allowed me to explore what I believed and valued while trusting that I would still have some solid base to my life even if I had to discard a lot of what I had accumulated in my earlier years. I felt very shaky at times as I surveyed those beliefs and assumptions but I always took comfort when I visualized the image of the firm, deep roots of my soul. I trusted those roots as I laid out my beliefs, discarding some, rearranging others, and gradually accepting what I perceived to be basic to my life. I also grew in being comfortable with gray areas and with questions that did not have answers. This growth was another one of the blessings of going deeper.

Midlife: A Call to Go Within

I did not know at the time of my desert experience that the journey to the interior is an essential part of the midlife process. I learned from my own journey, and from others, that interiority is an in-escapable dimension of growth for those who choose to respond to the midlife call. This movement into the unknown territory of our lives is an invitation to explore the vast interior of our psyche where many treasures are waiting to be found in the unconscious. A male respondent compared this to the image of a mine where "secrets, difficulties, wonderment, and decisions" are found (Q.R. — Questionnaire Response).[3] Author Sue Monk Kidd recognizes this call as she asks these questions:

> Is it possible, I asked myself, that I'm being summoned from some deep and holy place within? Am I being asked to enter a passage in the spiritual life — the journey from false self to true self? Am I being asked to dismantle old masks and patterns and unfold a deeper, more authentic self — the one God created me to be? Am I being compelled to disturb my inner universe in quest of the undiscovered being who clamors from within?[4]

While it may be more natural for the introverted person to go inward, the extroverted person is also drawn in this direction. It is here in the deeper part of us, Jung said, that a person goes when there is great work that needs to be done.[5] Thus, midlife involves a significant spiritual and psychological change in direction: from an externally oriented world to an internally oriented one. Midlife persons use numerous images to describe this inward journey: cave, well, forest, womb, cocoon, desert, tunnel, black hole, seeds in soil, roots of trees. . . . A female respondent noted that "the miracle of a tree is that it grows only as high as its roots are grounded deep in the earth" while another commented: "My midlife spirituality has changed from the linear, shallow, external one of my youth into a more internal and expansive journey — a source of energy" (Q.R.).

One respondent described this transition as being like that of a huge ocean liner ponderously and laboriously trying to turn itself in a vast sea. It can't turn quickly or with speed or make a sharp turn but turn it must. It takes time to move this unyielding ship and when we finally do so we have no idea where we are going! (Q.R.). This turning is a move toward the interior of one's life. Even if we have faithfully and regularly visited this inner sanctuary, we will be called inward again, deeper and further than we have ever traveled before.

To use another ship image, midlife is like being on the sea of life. We have been in a safe, secure yacht in which we knew all the nooks and crannies, had learned how to use all the instruments. It is comfy and cozy in there amid the tossing to and fro on the sea. Then, midlife comes along and we look around and see what we have in our boat. We begin to evaluate what we carry with us: our "shoulds," "oughts," "musts," "want to's." We see that what we carry on board is not enough. Something is lacking and it is to be found in the sea beneath the boat.

We stand on the edge of the boat and we dive into the waters. It takes awhile to get used to being in there. As we go deeper, we start finding all sorts of things. Some of it is the junk of old wounds that comes to the surface and needs to be let go while other discoveries are wonderful treasures that gift us with joy. As we explore these waters, we meet strange occupants in the deeps, some of which are frightening and others enigmatically beautiful and enticing.

Yet another image of going deeper is that used by William Bridges. He describes this movement in Hindu terms — going from the householder to the forest-dweller stage of life. The first half of life has been focused on the external part of self: work, raising a family and/or forming significant relationships, making money, being successful, living our dreams to "be someone." The second half of life, Bridges tells us, is meant to take us inward.[6] It is here, at the core or center of who we are, that we explore the immense and elusive truth of the Self. This journey holds its own perils and travails, but it is meant for us if greater wholeness is to be found.

One woman spoke to this issue when she described how she had no time for anything but the essentials of life when she had two children within eighteen months. She wrote, "I considered the day a success when I was dressed by afternoon!" She added, "I think that mothering can also mean less focus on one's own essential inner growth. Could that be why some empty-nesters are so devastated? They've not had time to tend the inner life and suddenly it is there before them, demanding their attention?" (Q.R.).

The movement from householder to forest-dweller is reflected in the comments of this woman:

> I felt a strong sense of a need to discover who I really was and what I had to offer life. I began to turn myself inward and discovered a reality I had never known — a timeless part of myself....I now feel the excitement of turning a bend in a forest path to discover a beautiful vista before me — waiting to be explored. (Q.R.)

The forest-dweller of the second half of life goes into the darkness and solitude in the same way one who dives deep into the sea goes into the unknown. I recall being in an Australian rain forest where, even in the daytime, the sun barely pierced through the dense cover of green. In the forest of midlife, there is also dense, tangled foliage that one must walk through. It is done in solitude. We go alone into that forest to discover how to find nourishment, how to protect and care well for self as the heavy rainstorms come and go, as the night brings uncomfortable darkness, and unknown creatures stir and travel in the inner woods.

Whether it is in the deep waters of the ocean or in the tangled, wet world of the rain forest, it is in the deepening places of ourselves that we find the treasures of truth that will nourish, guide, and sustain us as we move into the future. It is also in these deep places that we will face great obstacles. One of these obstacles is fear. Another is a refusal to accept the truth that we find. Another is impatience. Yet another is an unwillingness or an inability to let go and not to be in control for a time. Each midlife person has her or his own obstacle course. The challenge is to stay on the inner path and not turn back, to trust that there will be a Sacred Guide who will protect us and provide the safety we need so that we will not be destroyed or lost forever on that challenging sojourn of exploring the inner terrain of ourselves.[7]

This beckoning to wholeness, the discovery and acceptance of the missing pieces within one's self, is the process that C. G. Jung called "individuation." It involves not only going deeper and reclaiming the lost or unknown pieces of ourselves (the Shadow) but also accepting the dying that goes with this discovery. Our ego, that part of us that is conscious and thinks it knows everything, has either to relinquish some of its supposed truth (its illusions), or to give way to a much larger picture of what truth is. Our ego knows only a small portion of who we are.

There is so much deep within that cries out to be known and accepted. This process of diving into the unknown waters of the unconscious involves not only recognition but also acceptance of our deeper findings. As we accept these new pieces of self, a truer, more complete picture of the self emerges. We unite what we have known on the outside of ourselves with what we discover on the inside of ourselves.

Some midlife respondents referred to this process as finding the pieces to the puzzle of who they are. Before midlife, they thought that they had all of the pieces and it was just a matter of time before the pieces would fit together. To their dismay they discovered in midlife that some of the pieces they thought would fit together actually did not. Other pieces fit very well and there were some surprising ones that they had not even thought of seeking that were essential to their life's "picture."

Jesuit paleontologist Pierre Teilhard de Chardin insisted that we must try to penetrate our most secret self:

> And so, for the first time in my life...I took the lamp and, leaving the zone of everyday occupations and relationships where everything seems clear, I went down into my inmost self, to the deep abyss whence I feel dimly that my power of action emanates. But as I moved further and further away from the conventional certainties by which social life is superficially illuminated, I became aware that I was losing contact with myself. At each step of the descent a new person was disclosed within me of whose name I was no longer sure, and who no longer obeyed me. And when I had to stop my exploration because the path faded from beneath my steps, I found a bottomless abyss at my feet, and out of it came — arising I know not from where — the current which I dare to call *my* life.[8]

Teilhard de Chardin then tells of how he wanted to return to things as normal after his discovery, "to begin living again at the surface without imprudently plumbing the depths of the abyss," to forget about the disturbing things within, but he could not.[9] He had discovered his own soul with its depths and mystery and had become aware of his oneness with all of life. This truth changed him forever.

This process of going deeper continues throughout the rest of our lives. No matter how much hidden treasure we uncover, there is still more for us to reclaim. Whether the midlife move to the "within" of ourselves is a walk into a tangled forest, a turning of an old ship at sea, a deliberate effort to mine our treasures, or a diving into the deep waters, there will always be a call to discover more of the unknown. The later years of our life may not be as intense a movement inward but they will always invite us to more. We will continually be offered greater meaning and depth beyond what we have already discovered even though "nothing" may seem to be happening within us.

Simmering Time

I like food that is flavorful. Simmering food slowly, for a long time, helps the juices penetrate the whole. Hardly anyone simmers anything anymore. Everything is zapped in the microwave or cooked as quickly as possible. I think this reflects our spiritual life as well. Wisdom and wholeness deepen in us when we reflectively allow ideas and feelings to sit inside us for awhile. Thus, I offer simmering times at the end of each chapter. These are suggestions to help integrate the theme and images of the chapter.

These simmering times can be used in a variety of ways: (a) After reading the chapter, choose several of the exercises and record them in a journal. (b) Meet with a trusted companion to dialogue about what you have read and recorded. (c) Form a small midlife group. Meet after each chapter has been read and processed individually. Do one of the exercises together and/or use the questions for discussion. (Suggestions for a brief ritual at these gatherings are in Appendix D, p. 168.)

~

1. Which image suggested in this chapter most speaks to your own midlife process of going inward? Is there an image from your life that speaks more fully to this experience?

~

2. Set aside time to ponder your inner journey. Allow at least twenty minutes to be still. Be attentive to your breathing as you begin this quiet time. Let surface whatever comes. After twenty minutes, take up your journal and write a dialogue between you and your true Self. Ask your true Self a question that arises from your depths such as: How open am I to going deeper? What do I need to continue my inward journey? Am I afraid of anything as I go deeper? Is there something to which I need to be especially attentive?

~

3. Your roots:

   a. Reflect upon the roots of your life.

   - Write down your key beliefs and assumptions, those "inner statements and messages" that formed a foundation for your attitudes and behaviors before you entered midlife.

   - Look at these from your midlife perspective. Which ones have you discarded? Which ones have you rearranged or adjusted?

   - Now reflect on the new beliefs/assumptions that are developing or have begun to take root.

   b. After this reflection, draw a tree with roots to symbolize your central beliefs and assumptions today.

   - Look at your roots. What are they like? Going deep? thick? wobbly and thin? secure? sturdy? stretching out? ...?

   - What do these roots tell you about your beliefs and assumptions?

   c. On the roots, jot words and phrases that indicate what your central beliefs and assumptions are now.

   d. You may want to dialogue with your roots or with a particular belief or assumption.

~

4. Search within to see if you have any fears of going inward. If you have some fears, list these. Ask each fear what it wants of you. Let the fears know what you are, or are not, willing to give them.

~

5. Thomas Merton wrote:

> This true inner self must be drawn up
> like a jewel from the bottom of the sea... [10]

Lie on your back quietly. Encourage yourself to be in as receptive a posture as possible. Call for your angel or spiritual guide to be with you. See yourself taking a journey inward. Go slowly with your guide into the long tunnel. Sense the protection of your guide. Continue until you come to the Light. It is there, deep within you. Explore what you find. Look for the jewels. Describe to your guide what you see. Dialogue with your guide about this. Then slowly return to the present moment. Let yourself continue to relax. Take up your pen, or your paints and brush, or your clay, and record what you have experienced.

~

6. *Questions for journaling and/or discussion:*

- Did you ever feel a call to "go deeper"? If so, how did this happen? When did it come? How has it progressed in your life? Where has it led you? What have you learned?

- What has changed the most for you on your inner journey?

- What would you tell someone else about the inner journey of midlife?

~

7. Tend to the divine presence by sitting in stillness for awhile. Write a reflection about "going deeper."

~

A Prayer for Going Deeper

O Divine Presence,
I do not enter the deeper realm
all by myself.
Always you are there with me
as a Guide to protect and direct me,
as a Loving Companion to embrace and support me,
as a Wise One to provide both challenge and solace.

O Divine Presence,
as I go deeper to discover my roots,
wrap me in your love.
Strengthen me as I face fear and insecurity,
surprise me with hidden treasures
waiting within me.

O Divine Presence,
when I feel shaky and uncertain
from seeking and searching,
assure me often
that I am always rooted in your love.
Remind me often
that your love never leaves me,
even when I lose the road
to my inner home.

O Divine Presence,
you desire my wholeness.
You would never lead me anywhere
that would destroy me.
Here is my life.
I place it in your care
as I commit myself to going deeper.

—Joyce Rupp

CHAPTER TWO

Midlife Darkness: Entering the Cave

The Cave is the place of rebirth, that secret cavity in which
one is shut up in order to be incubated and renewed.

—C. G. JUNG

December mornings
hang in the air,
like a black mantle
wrapped around the earth.

I wait to walk
until the blue-gray dawn
slowly shapes silhouettes
on poplar branches.

this darkness
I do not mind.
I know the earth
keeps turning,
that lighter days
will linger soon.

it is the long days
inside my heart
that disturb me.
they have no season,
no calendar to turn.
they do not end
with the dawn
or lift
with the spring.

in the dark days
of my heart
I do not wait to walk
until light lingers
for I know not
when it shall come.

I go instead
stumbling into darkness,
searching for a road,
straining to see a way.

darkness —
it is the place
of growth,
and I am ripe for it.

                                        —JOYCE RUPP

WHEN WE SAY YES to the midlife journey of going deeper, we say yes to the possibility of being in the darkness. This darkness comes in many forms and patterns. It can be a brief visitor or a long-term resident. I have had many times of darkness. Just when I thought I would no longer live in the land of gloom and uncertainty, another call to darkness would come upon me. The darkness held a variety of emotions, none of which felt good. Yet, in the deepest part of me, I knew that these unwanted visitors were a necessary part of my becoming more whole. Oftentimes my darkness was not pitch-black. Rather, the color within me was more blah or dull, lethargic, with little energy or vitality:

gray-white
so wears the world
this November day
gray-white
so wears my soul
this November day
I rise out of duty
I move out of habit
I go forth out of necessity

gray-white —
how long will I wear it?

taste the sadness
bring the full cup
to the lips of the heart
imbibe slowly
for it tastes rank and bitter

> taste the pain
> bring the cup again
> to lips that resist it
> pour it into the soul
> let it circulate the sorrow
> it needs to sit and ferment
> let it be, let it be. (P. J.)

One of the most profound dreams I've ever had consisted of one simple image and six letters. I saw a cave with a door on which there were three letters: "wol." Next to the cave door were three more letters: "lof." When I wrote the letters in my journal, I realized that they spelled "follow" backward. This dream was the beginning of another period of profound growth. I had known for a long time that I was being called to stay in the darkness and learn from it, but until this "cave door" dream I never felt so intensely compelled or motivated. I finally came to the point of knowing that there was truly no other way but to go to the inner depths and stay in that dark space of the cave. (My first cave image had occurred nearly fifteen years earlier.)

The cave has long been symbolic of the inner psyche, a place of withdrawal and reflection, the space where new life and nurturance develops. Caves can be dark, smelly, bat-infested, dank, wet, and murky but they can also be nurturing, warm, sheltering havens for hibernation, gestation, and protection. Caves have been used as aging or maturing places for wines and storage places for vegetables, fruits, and dried flowers. Thus, the cave is a very dynamic image of the move inward where transformation happens. It is an image of the space where smelly, musty weaknesses are recognized and claimed, where gestation and birthing of newness occurs, where the wisdom of our earlier years is ripened and matured, where we can seek shelter and protection from the storms of life's strife, and where we can go to ponder and reflect on what has taken place outside the cave.[1]

There are marvelous movements of growth that take place in the cave of our unconscious, but it is not always easy to be in this cave with its dark, unknown nooks and crannies where we are unable to find the light switch. There are no well-formed paths in a cave. We find our way in this mysterious realm through searching step by step, feeling the damp walls and listening to the rustling of wings and the noise of little creatures, all the while constantly renewing our trust that we will be safe.

The "cave" is about darkness, depression, silence, pain, waiting, not knowing, fear, struggle, obstacles, and all those things one wants to avoid in life by staying constantly preoccupied with the external world. The cave is the place to be if we want to grow and are willing to know suffering and purification. The cave is about nurturing life. Bursts of insight, grieving that aids healing, and seeds of truth for future guidance are some of the gifts of the cave time.

My earliest encounter with the image of the cave was in my thirty-first year. I was making my first eight-day retreat, which included total silence. I was not ready for the silence, and I found the days both excruciatingly long and hollow. I wrote in my journal on the last day of that retreat:

> I still feel wanting and incomplete. Is this what it is like to experience the cave? I want to accept the cave with its darkness, loneliness, and emptiness. I feel lost. Where do I turn? What do I do? How do I go? (P.J.)

It's probably a good thing that I did not know then that this was the beginning of a twenty-year movement, continuously in and out of the cave. Two years after the dreadful retreat experience, I made this entry:

> Deep is calling unto deep. Stop standing before the dark, empty cave. Take a step. Let go. Walk in. Just like the seed must fall into the dark, deep black soil, so must I enter into the darkness, go where there is mystery, where the questions float without answers. My steps are slow but I move into the unknown. I cry out in the cave. My voice echoes on the walls as it flies through the emptiness. Silence. This

deep demands silence. The long wait begins. All seems futile. Useless. Silly. Meaningless. Why deliberately walk into a hollow, empty, silent darkness? Deep within me a tiny voice whispers the truth: "If you want to grow you must die to self. Here in the place of darkness you will learn what life is. You will find an energy that you've never dreamed possible. You will know a transformation that shall dazzle the eyes of your spirit. Come, go deep. It is worth it. Do not forget this journey. It is meant for you. Love it. It is your source of transformation." (P. J.)

I would remember the cave for awhile and be attentive to the journey. Then, my life would get full of many things and being in the cave would get put aside unless the sense of darkness was too powerful to be avoided. I was very much like a bear, going into the cave to hibernate, then coming out, feeding and enjoying the sunshine, then going back into the cave again for another long winter. A year after the above journal entry, I wrote:

I am in a dark, damp cave. I can see nothing. Vague images of shelves with fruit jars. I can only feel my way to discover what is there. I'm afraid to touch anything out of fear that I will get hurt or maybe come across something that's foreign or unknown. I keep standing in there. I feel damp and dirty. I can hardly breathe. I resist the temptation to walk over to the light switch. This is my lesson of walking in the dark again. There is something to be learned, something very, very significant only I can't get at it. Again, I turn to you, God, and ask you to grant me the vision to see in the dark, to know what it is that creates desolation and turmoil deep within me. (P. J.)

This need to be in the cave kept pursuing me. I wrote about feeling like I was in the fallow-time, about "the long black shadows of life blocking the light of my stumbling journey." The image of "womb" also filled the pages of my journal. I thought of it synonymously with cave — a dark, unknown place of waiting where something would be birthed. My dreams often held night-time scenes and dark roads. Over and over I kept hearing this reassurance from within: "Stay in the Dark."

While I had a sense that something would be birthed from the darkness, I also knew that darkness could be painful and full of emotions I did not want, such as discouragement, doubt, and sadness. At times the darkness felt as though all the dreams in me had died:

> Today is the darkest day of the year. Lately I've felt many darkest days in my heart and the strong sense that my dreams are lost and even worse, that I ought not to look for them — instead, that I need to walk in the bleakness and feel my way through the fearful blindness, stumbling around in my life until I discover some new vision that's meant to embrace me. It's hard enough to walk around in the darkness when the flame of a dream burns inside but when the light of that goal also fades the journey seems perilous and overwhelming. (P. J.)

In my "cave door" dream, I was standing in front of the cave door looking out, reading "follow," and realizing that I had to turn around and go inside. I felt that I had already spent enough time in the darkness. Why was I being called to go in again? Was there yet more to be revealed? (Of course, there was, and always is.) A part of me was fearful of doing this again and another part of me realized that it was an honor and a privilege for my psyche to be extending this invitation. I was becoming more and more convinced of the value of the darkness of the cave even though I still didn't like being there.

A day after the cave door dream, I read, "The abundance of the sea will be brought to you" (Is 60:5). I was stunned with these words, with the synchronicity of finding them, knowing that the sea was a strong symbol for the unconscious. The call to go into the cave of the unknown was being confirmed. For the first time in my life, I didn't feel like fighting the journey. I *wanted* to go inside to discover what the treasure would be. I sensed that this journey would be one of ripening and maturing.

My "cave door" dream was a blessing dream for me, confirming what was taking place in my spiritual journey. I was forty-seven years old at the time of this dream. I wasn't in the throes of deep depression or in a crisis. But I did feel that all the old maps that used to give me direction just didn't work anymore. I felt lost in many areas of my life. My church and cultural issues with patriarchy rumbled loudly. Yet, I also saw that I had some of those same tendencies in my life. My drive for success, efficiency, and control seemed to violate my deep desire for contemplation, beauty, and solitude. I sensed a certain void in me. My persona, the "person" I showed to the world, was also hanging on to me like a tattered dress. I wasn't sure that I wanted to continue being the person that others knew. Yes, it was definitely cave-time for me.

As I entered the cave once more, I allowed myself to fall into an emptiness of heart where all the old maps that used to give me such good direction in life faded and fell apart. I had to be at home there in order to see in a new way, in order to find an inner direction that I could discover only in the darkness. I needed to nurture and care for the deepest part of my Self so that something yet unknown could be birthed.

Since the time of the dream I have identified parts of my psyche that were lost and in need of finding, empty places that yearned to be filled, crowded spots that had to have things tossed out, anger that needed attention, sadness that longed to be comforted and consoled. All of this I found, and am still finding, by being faithful to the cave that calls for solitude, acceptance of not-knowing, attentiveness to stillness, and the discipline of daily reflection.

Two years after the "cave door dream" I had another powerful dream. It consisted of one image: a dragon. I had the sense that the dragon was welcoming and wise.[2] In active imagination, I entered a cave and walked a long way, down many, many steps to a huge cavern in the earth. It was quite dark on the way down, but when I reached the interior I met again this marvelous dragon of my dream. I knew she had been waiting for me. She sat before a pool of clear water. The dragon beckoned for me to sit by her right side, on her large, green paw. I could feel a sort of welcoming caress by her. I sat there quietly. She held a book. "WISDOM" was written on the cover. She opened it for me to read.

As I looked into the book of WISDOM I realized that it was written in dragon language and I could not read it. But I kept looking and looking at the page until finally, I could see what it said: "BRING BACK THE CHILD!" These words brought tears because they spoke so deeply to my soul. I realized that this was one of the major things that needed retrieving in the cave of my self — the Child of spontaneous emotions, the Child of play and creativity, the Child who wanted the freedom to be herself rather than keep attending to the expectations of her adult world.

I left the dragon that day but returned to her many times. One day I went to her with my concerns about continuing to be in the cave. As I sat in the crook of her arm, I began singing in a child's voice, telling her my fears, worries, and concerns. I told her that I was afraid of not knowing the way in the dark and of losing my way, that I felt insecure and lonely. I gave her my struggles with being too responsible and too production-oriented in my life. I let her know that I was concerned about what others would think of me if I were to change and that I might look stupid, foolish, or crazy. I told the dragon everything. She, in turn, kept calling to me: "Come, come into the cave, into the Dark, into the Unknown." She assured me that I needed to stay in the dark if I wanted to grow.[3]

Darkness has helped me to trust the process of midlife growth and to let go of preconceived theories and expectations about the way life is, about what I thought I couldn't live without, and who I thought I had to be. Darkness has taught me to be less afraid of the unknown and actually to relish it because I now know from experience that the unconscious has much to offer me for my growth.

Darkness has also helped me to feel more compassionately united with each piece of the universe. It has helped me drop my pretensions and to see that the Source of life unites us. We are all in this together. Darkness has also given me greater ability to listen and to feel safe in solitude, where so many treasures lie. I have learned to wait and I have learned that all my growthful journeys include many visits to the cave.

Midlife and Darkness

The cave was not only a significant image for my midlife process; it was also a key image for some of the respondents. They too, recognized that midlife offers the opportunity for personal transformation while usually demanding some time spent in the darkness. One man said that he returned again and again to the biblical image of Elijah spending the night in a cave. He could identify immensely with Elijah's experience of hearing God say to him: "Elijah, what are you doing here?" (1 Kgs 19:9) (Q.R.).

One woman wrote that the cave image "describes perfectly a very difficult period of darkness, silence, and pain. I remember the musty storage space under a mountain cabin we owned when I was a child. There were old trunks filled with wonderful treasures but it was necessary to go into the dark space with spiders and who knows what else in order to find the treasures. That describes my midlife struggle" (Q.R.).

These dark and lonely spaces of the cave often contain depression as the structure of one's well-built world tumbles apart and is slowly rebuilt. This aspect of darkness includes a profound suffering that is difficult to describe but that is felt intensely by the one experiencing it. One respondent named this "the tomb of numbness...the void of emptiness" (Q.R.).

May Sarton contends that many will not accept suffering as a part of transformation. She insists: "We fear disturbance, change, fear to bring to light and to talk about what is painful. Suffering often feels like failure, but is actually the door into growth. And growth does not cease to be painful at any age."[4] Sometimes this suffering is the pain of not knowing, of having to let go of clinging to the light and learning to befriend the darkness of depression. A female respondent used the image of the tomb to describe her struggle with this darkness:

On the threat of the recurring darkness of depression, I fled
to the "light." Still the darkness called to me, pursued me.
I ran! — in activity, work, family, reading, anything! About
eight months ago I stopped running and turned to face the
dark — it was calling my name. During a meditation, Jesus
took me into the tomb (the womb of the earth), wrapped me
in burial cloth and laid me on the slab. I was told to stay
there...and there I am!...One of the things I have prayed
for is for God to call my name and then, this darkness called
my name. Yet, I didn't recognize it as God. (Q.R.)

I have found both comfort and challenge in the writings of those
who have delved into the darkness of transformation. These writers
often refer to this journey into the unknown as a "descent" into
darkness. They use a variety of images to describe it: a journey to
the underworld, the night-sea journey, the wilderness or desert, the
dark night of the soul, the belly of the whale, the descent, or the
meeting of the dark goddess.

Jungian analyst and author Murray Stein uses Hermes as the
predominant figure in his work *In Midlife.* Hermes, the god of
transitions and magic, is well-known for his mischief and thiev-
ery. Stein sees Hermes, the cave-dweller, as an "inventive force"
within the midlife person that asserts itself and demands attention.
Hermes disrupts life, throws one off-balance, steals the treasure
to which the midlife person is so attached (ego-identity with its
security), and offers new gifts from the unconscious.[5]

Stein notes that in midlife there is a "crossing over from one
psychological identity to another."[6] He calls this crossing over a
time of "liminality" and uses the image of a limen, which is
the threshold, or opening, or the in-between place of a door-
way, to depict what happens as "a person's sense of identity is
hung in suspension."[7] When we are in this "liminality" it is as
though we are homeless, standing in the in-between, not knowing
where we are going. He warns that during this time of liminality
the inner ground shifts and, because the base is not firm, a person can be very vulnerable, "easily influenced, pushed, and blown

about."[8] There is a time of darkness and unsureness when one passes through the door of liminality to confront repressed elements and accept the valuable experience of "the burial of a former sense of self."[9] During this period, we need to be especially caring of ourselves.

Joseph Campbell speaks of this descent as an "initiation" into the dark of the unconscious. He envisioned it as "a call to adventure" in which one detaches or withdraws from the external to the internal world. Campbell based his image on C. G. Jung's notion of transformation as "the night-sea journey," where one moves into the sea of the unconscious to discover what is needed for the second half of life.[10] Jean Shinoda Bolen also sees the element of darkness in personal growth and notes that most transformative journeys "involve going through a dark place" and finally emerging into light.[11]

Although Joseph Campbell insists that the heroic journey is that of both men and women, Maureen Murdock finds subtle differences between men's and women's cave-time. She sees women embracing a stereotypical male heroic journey (being caught in being productive and successful) when, in fact, what women actually need to do is to recover their own lost feminine.[12] For women this means a voluntary or an involuntary descent to the inner world.[13] This period of withdrawal may come without the person knowing why. It involves a time of isolation — "a period of darkness and silence and of learning the art of deeply listening once again to the self: of *being* instead of doing."[14]

One woman respondent wrote of this significant move through darkness as being freed "from the chains and claims of the past." She also compared it to "the tingling of a thaw, with glaciers moving away from my heart, allowing it to be softened and mended by love's energy." She felt that she had been through a long, dark period and was finally more "anchored in peace"(Q.R.).

This journey of darkness to light, from death to life, is the pattern of the Jewish story of the Exodus. In it the people are held in the darkness of slavery in Egypt. They then wander in the desert for a symbolic forty years (meaning a *long, long time*) before discovering the Promised Land. Similarly, the darkness of transformation is symbolized in the Christ journey of death on the cross, entombment, and then resurrection. Everywhere in life and in the scriptures the necessity for the dark time is central to transformation.

Mythology also offers many stories that include the descent into darkness as an essential element for personal transformation. The involuntary descent of the Greek goddess Persephone is one of these myths which speaks to midlife. In this myth, Persephone is forced to go down with Hades, god of the underworld, and is not allowed to return until she agrees to spend one-half of the rest of her life in the darkness of the underworld. This myth originally spoke of the seasons of winter and summer, but it also brings with it the deeper level of the seasons of our lives that tell us that we too must spend a certain amount of inner growth in the winter of darkness.

Birth is a key image connected with darkness. It is in the cave that the mother bear gives birth to her young. Numerous respondents referred to some inner movements "from darkness to light" as a part of their process. They used images from nature where there is always a gestation period that involves darkness, loss of control, and waiting for birth: the chrysalis as it forms the butterfly; the seed planted in the dark earth waiting for a new, green shoot; the gestation in the womb before the birth of a child.

Darkness often brings its own set of formidable obstacles or tests that are given in order to release the capacities and hidden strengths of the individual. Perils are found along the way through this dying and birthing, and thus there is usually fear and resistance toward going into the unknown realms of darkness. The midlife adult may recognize that this descent into the underworld or into the cave is necessary but fights it all the same. Marian Woodman asks:

> Why are we so afraid of change? Why, when we are so desperate for change, do we lose our childhood faith in growing? Why do we cling to old attachments instead of submitting

ourselves to new possibilities — to the undiscovered worlds in our own bodies, minds and souls?[15]

She goes on to write that the great fear of being destroyed or annihilated by this journey to the depths of darkness is due to our Western emphasis on linear growth and achievement rather than the benefits that come from going deep within oneself. Our extroverted world rarely supports introverted withdrawal. This has a definite influence on midlife adults when they come face to face with the possibility of spending time in the cave.

Whatever image is used to express the journey into darkness, going deeper is never easy. In this place of rebirth, we must keep hope that there is something vital and valuable going on within us. The cave time is a beckoning to see things never before known to us. Like the stars, these hidden treasures can be revealed only in the dark of night. In midlife we need to trust these cave times and restore our belief in the value of midnight adventures.

Simmering Time

1. Which image of darkness in this chapter most speaks to your own midlife process of experiencing darkness? Is there an image from your life that more fully expresses your experience of darkness?

~

2. Set aside time to ponder your experience of darkness. If possible, do this in a darkened room without any lights on. Allow at least twenty minutes to sit in the darkness. Notice what thoughts and feelings arise. Be aware of memories that surface. Are there any fears of the darkness? After you have been in the darkness for twenty or more minutes, light a candle. Be with this light as you reflect on your experience of sitting in the darkness.

~

3. Questions for journaling and/or discussion:

- Have you experienced a significant time of darkness?

- If yes, what was this like for you?

- What do you most resist about the cave of darkness?

- Do you care for yourself when you are in darkness? (If so, how?)

- What gives you the courage to go on?

- How would you respond to someone who was in the midst of inner darkness?

~

4. Take some quiet time to reflect on your life experience of light and darkness. How do you feel about these two aspects of growth? Which dimension is more predominant in your life now? Take your paints or markers and draw your experience of light and darkness.

~

5. How has darkness been a teacher for you? Make a list of your significant times of darkness. Next to each one, describe what you have learned from each experience of darkness.

~

6. Ponder this verse from Rabindranath Tagore's poetry:

> Only in the deepest silence of night
> the stars smile and whisper among themselves.[16]

Dance the verse, or draw it, or sing it, or have it come alive in clay.

~

7. Sit outdoors at dusk on a clear-sky evening. Be with the earth as the night slowly comes. Let the stars smile and whisper their truths to you. What might the stars' song be for you? If you hear this melody, hum it for awhile.

~

A Prayer for the Cave Time

Guardian of my soul, thank you,
for guiding me in the dark places,
for reaching me through the people of my life,
for drawing near to love me when I feel unlovable,
for teaching me how to tend my wounds,
for guarding me with words of truth
and moments of empowerment,
for allowing my pain and struggle
so that I can come to greater wholeness.

Guardian of my soul,
you are my Coach in the Cave,
my Voice in the Fog,
my Midwife of Wisdom.
I place my trust in you
as I give myself to the process
of learning from my darkness.

—Joyce Rupp

CHAPTER THREE

*Midlife Searching:
Old Maps No Longer Work*

*Somewhere down the road we suddenly look for and can no
longer find what belongs to us or to what we belong. Then
our sense of soul is mysteriously missing, and more so, it is
hidden away. And so we wander about partially dazed.*

—Clarissa Pinkola Estes

I keep pulling it out —
the old map of my inner path.
I squint closely at it,
trying to see some hidden road
that maybe I've missed,
but there's nothing there now
except some well-traveled paths.
they have seen my footsteps often,
held my laughter, caught my tears.

I keep going over the old map
but now the roads lead nowhere,
a meaningless wilderness
where life is dull and futile.

"toss away the old map," she says.
"you must be kidding!" I reply.
she looks at me with Sarah eyes
and repeats, "toss it away.
it's of no use where you're going."

"I have to have a map!" I cry,
"even if it takes me nowhere.
I can't be without direction."
"but you are without direction,"
she says, "so why not let go, be free?"

so there I am — tossing away the old map,
sadly, fearfully, putting it behind me.
"whatever will I do?" wails my security.
"trust me" says my midlife soul.

no map. no specific directions.
no "this way ahead" or "take a left."
how will I know where to go?
how will I find my way? no map!
but then my midlife soul whispers:
"there was a time before maps
when pilgrims traveled by the stars."

> it is time for the pilgrim in me
> to travel in the dark,
> to learn to read the stars
> that shine in my soul.
> I will walk deeper
> into the dark of my night,
> I will wait for the stars,
> trust their guidance,
> and let their light be enough for me.
>
> — JOYCE RUPP

I WAS VERY NEW to hiking in the mountains when I got lost one day. It was my first time to venture out by myself on an unknown trail. I felt exhilarated and knew nothing of the dangers or of the care and caution that one needs to take. I made the mistake of moving off the trail and not marking the spot where I left it when I went into an inviting section of the forest. I was enthralled with the odor of the pines and the softness of the needles underneath the trees. I walked rather aimlessly until I heard a boom of thunder and saw a flash of lightning. Panic set in. I fled down the hill through the trees and could not find the path. Rain began pelting me and the thunder sounded ever closer. Finally, I found the path, but by then I was so confused from dashing about in the trees that I did not know if I ought to go to the left or to the right. I had lost all sense of direction. Nothing looked familiar either way. When I did make the decision to go to the left, I had no idea where the path would take me. Fortunately, I had chosen the path that led back to the cabin.

Feeling lost, losing my sense of direction, experiencing panic, searching for the way to go, hoping to find a familiar path, finding my way home — all this has been a part of my midlife experience. Midlife has been a continual process of getting terribly lost inside, feeling far away from who I am, from the space of "me," struggling and yearning to come home to myself and then, all of a sudden, feeling at home, finding a space in me that I had either forgotten or newly discovered.

Sometimes my lost-ness had the quality of hunting for intuited inner riches. One day I wrote: "I am searching for some unknown treasure, hidden in the field of life, to be found only with your skilled direction, God. It must be you who stirs me so, who urges me along even when I feel terribly lost" (P.J.). Intuitively, I knew that I had other qualities to live and that there were other ways for me to approach my life, but I was unable to envision these things. I simply had this sense of "something more."

I have felt lost in my relationship to God, wondered who this God was, and how to name this God. I've wandered around as a woman in the Roman Catholic Church trying to find a place for myself. I've searched for a link in my relationship with others and wondered who I wanted to spend the rest of my life with in friendship and whether or not I wanted to remain in my religious community. I've felt lost in my work when things were a mess and when I wondered if I needed to move on to something else. When inundated with the cares of others, I have lost my enthusiasm and verve for life.

A sense of fear and dread about the "unnamed" often crept into me when I felt challenged to stretch and to grow, to risk some new behavior or idea, or to reach out toward something that still felt foreign or alien to my belief system or personal experience. I remember feeling the comfort of kinship on the day that I turned a page of Jessica Powers's poetry and came to the poem in which she describes Abraham as "that old weather-beaten, unwavering nomad" who was called to a strange, unknown territory. Powers comments on her own "far and lonely journey" that led her to "take out old maps and stare."[1]

I could easily picture the scene of Abraham looking at all the accumulations of his life that had given him security and ease. I could see how he might think that moving into a strange, distant land was a ridiculous idea. He must have valued his old maps: his style of life, his process of thinking, his way of action. Why would he leave all that for something that had the smell of danger and the goose-bumps of a map-less terrain? Abraham is, of course, a symbol of a part of ourselves. The mystic Jessica Powers obviously knew this "Abraham experience" on an interior level of her life. I have known it, too. There have been significant instances when everything in me wanted to cling to the "old maps" instead of opening up to the unknown, unmapped territory of my growth. This has been particularly true for me when I have needed to let go of my secure way of imaging and relating to God and when I have struggled with that basic question: "Who am I?"[2]

I understand my desire to want to cling to "old maps." It is a normal human phenomenon. Almost everyone in the Hebrew and Christian scriptures wanted to hang on to what they knew. Even Mary of Nazareth asked questions and searched for direction before she said yes to the angel of God. I've often pondered the Israelites' exodus out of Egypt. As they moved into the wilderness they were eager to leave the chains of slavery that bound them, but as soon as they were in unknown territory, with no end in sight, they rose up and grumbled about how foolish the trip was, how they ought never to have left the land of Egypt. They insisted that they ought to turn around and go back — at least they knew what they had when they were in Egypt. Their old life kept them from freedom, but they would rather have gone back to that life than to face the unsettling challenges of the wilderness before them. Yes, I know that feeling of taking out the old maps and staring.

I have felt lost inside many times in my midlife trek. When this lost feeling pervaded, I knew that I was seeking for someone or something and, yet, I often did not know what it was that I hoped to find. The following entries were written in different years, but they speak of the same thing: being directionless.

I am *nowhere* (still feel disconnected, empty). I am somewhere. (I'm touching on some sort of truth.) I am anywhere. (This sounds like an old pattern of my life). (P. J.)

When I turn inside I feel like I've taken one step inside the door and immediately gotten lost. Where am I? It all looks like strange territory. I'm uncomfortable. I don't have any sense of direction. I feel all apart. (P. J.)

The sight of dormant branches helped me to name the lost-ness that slept inside of me. At age thirty-four lostness was already pursuing me:

> Last evening I looked out my early November window and tasted the salt of sudden tears. It was the burst of recognition that spun among my sadness: the sight of dormant branches. I saw my life lying there, flung out against the blue sky, wait-ing in bitter cold for something without a name. There's a dormant spot in my spirit that sleeps inside my energy. I want to rush and wake it up but it only lies in mystery. I ache with bits of longing and wish for eyes to know what it is that waits the wording. Ah, I feel like those barren branches. When will I ever know? (P.J.)

I found myself searching for who I was and how I was to be, longing for the freedom that comes with self-discovery:

> Recovering my true Self! I think that's what I yearn for. I feel bogged down, mired in, want to touch the spot that really feels like "me." Who or what takes hold of me? Who and what takes up inner energy? Am I about the right things? I feel so lost sometimes. No sense of wingedness. I want to fly and I know that I can (deep inside I do know this) but I seem only to plod along. What holds me down? I yearn to refind myself. (P.J.)

There have been periods of my midlife journey when I felt lost because I was somewhere between the old and the new and nothing seemed to fit. The old didn't wear well, and the new was either too uncomfortable or too masked with unknown possibili-ties. At times, it seemed like I lost a part of my heart. Sometimes I felt bewildered, disoriented, and uncentered. This confusion was unsettling and took away my peace:

> First day of March, month of spring, and I am feeling full of winter. Cold. Like a desert moved in over night. Barren. Like I took the wrong forest path. Really lost. Like I lost a part

of my heart. So many questions. I am full of "I don't know"
today, God. My faith seems low and weak. (P. J.)

There were also scary times when I was not only lost but could
not feel much of anything. My unfeelingness frightened me and
caused me to wonder if I'd ever feel again. The feelings did return.
It was a matter of waiting and trusting, believing that I had the
power within me to "return home."

I recall the time that I was in British Columbia participating in
a wilderness retreat. On the first evening that our group gathered,
we listened to the wilderness advice of a wise forest ranger named
Ferguson. He warned us about taking necessary clothing and pro-
visions in our packs, about staying on the trails, and what to do if
we were to get lost. "If you get lost," he said, "don't try to keep
finding the way out. Go a short ways off the trail by a tree. Wait
for someone to come and show you the way home. Whatever you
do, don't panic." The ranger assured us that he and his associate
knew those paths well and that they would come and find us. He
also commented that getting lost and waiting to be found could
be an "exalted" thing; one could get in touch with the woods and
earth, really look and see in a way that one would not when hiking
busily down the trail.

Those words found a sensitive place in me. The last thing I
wanted to do was get lost. Getting lost felt disastrous to me. I
wanted to have control of exactly where I was going. I didn't want
to lose sight of where I was or what was ahead. I certainly didn't
want to have to sit down, and just "be," while I relied on someone
else to come and find me and show me the way. This waiting to be
found challenged my independence, my desire to "go it alone," to
try to rationalize and figure it out, not to acknowledge being lost,
and to resist needing someone else who was wiser and more experienced to help me find my true Self. I secretly worried that I'd feel
shame or ineptness if they knew me as I truly was. When I sat on
my inner trail of life and felt lost, I didn't want anyone to know it.

Years later, I realized how wise the ranger's advice was, not only
for hikers, but also for midlife journeyers. I have gotten lost in the

mystery of who I am. I have needed a wise companion to help me find the way home to my true Self. I had to learn how to trust another with my lostness. Sometimes this wise companion was a close friend, sometimes a skilled therapist or spiritual director. Always it has been a turning to my Wise Companion, God, the One who says to me: "When you get lost, stop, wait, trust. I know the way. I will find you and lead you out." (I have often asked God to be good to the "stranger" in me and to show me the way to my inner home.) And, yes, it has been a most exalted time when I stopped to look deep and long at my inner world. I saw things that I missed entirely when I was fully in control, rushing down the trail of life.

Another piece of advice from the ranger also fit into my midlife journey. "Don't panic," the ranger had warned. Fear was a natural emotion that arose in me when I was lost or not sure of the future. When my world felt like dense fog, swirling duststorms, or a blizzard whiteout, anxiety quickly tried to take over. Fear can overpower me unless I stand up to it, face it, and not let it bully me around. Thus, I frequently wrote my fears in my journal as a means of both acknowledging and getting some distance from them.

Sometimes these fears were not so much about losing old maps as they were about how to live in the territory of a new map. There were times when I was ready to step off the well-worn road, to toss the old map away, but I feared making unwise decisions about the future. I remember a section of my midlife passage when I grew very doubtful about my vowed life in my religious community. The vows of celibacy, poverty, and obedience, which I had promised twenty-five years earlier, no longer seemed adequate. The outdated structures had changed but the old vision, based on a parent-child mode of relating, was deeply rooted.

While I struggled and stumbled around in my questions and my doubts, I also sought the help of a wise companion. She was my "forest ranger" helping me to find a way out. Instead of urging me to leave my community, she invited me to dream of a religious community the way I would envision it. What would it look like? What would give my vows meaning and substance? What would help me be psychologically and spiritually healthy? Was leaving my community the only option or was there a way for me to remain faithful but also be true to the growth that was occurring for me?

As I pondered her questions, I was able to see how my values were basically the same but my vision and my lived experience had changed tremendously. I discovered that the vows I'd promised had a new flavor to them. While I would retain my celibate state, the goal of this vow was not to be celibate but to be a compassion-ate woman, united in love with all of life. The vow of poverty was not poverty in a financial sense but a vow to simplicity on all levels. My vow of obedience moved from a hierarchical, au-thoritarian approach to one of community, where no one went to "superiors" for permissions. Rather, each was urged to seek the truth within herself and to make decisions based on the good of all members.

My new naming of the vows as compassion, simplicity, and community gave me an inner freedom. It felt like coming home. I knew that I could stand deep and strong in this truth that I had finally named even though others might not understand or agree with my perceptions. My letting go of the old maps didn't resolve all my struggles with my vowed commitment but it did give me a renewed rootedness, an internal empowerment that was not there before. I could walk into the new territory with hope.

As I reflect on the many times I've felt lost during my midlife journey, I recognize that I have come home to more and more of my true Self. Less and less of me feels lost. I have discovered how helpful the "forest rangers" can be and I have learned how to wait. I am also more willing to live with questions that have no immedi-ate answers. I am enjoying the process of my existence instead of having it all figured out. I am learning to live with fewer maps.

Midlife: Feeling Lost and Searching

The sense of being lost and searching is a common experience for many in midlife. We become spiritual nomads, wandering around hoping to discover an elusive something that defies a naming. Nothing satisfies. We are left longing for some missing pieces that we do not have and wonder if we will ever find. Being lost propels us in the direction of the discovery of new inner territory. This process involves looking intently at our supposed securities (our old maps), exploring the story of who we are and how life is, and searching for the roads that will lead us forward. It means trusting that we will find ourselves again.

Many midlife people who appear outwardly successful, who seem to "have it all together," actually feel as though they have a wilderness within them. They are not sure of who they are or what they want in life. No matter what occupation they have, it may not satisfy. No matter how much effort they put into spiritual, physical, or mental renewal, they can still feel an emptiness and a loneliness permeating their days. They can lose their sexual drive. They can spend endless emotional energy searching for something to stir the embers of a relationship that once pulsed with vitality. They can run frenzied into activity in search of themselves. As one respondent put it: "Sometimes I feel so lost. Where am I going? What will it mean when I get there? Why does growing have to be so hard?" (Q.R.).

One woman reflected that midlife was like a spiral, where it sometimes seems that one is going backward but is actually going forward. Another respondent described it as "a period of rudderlessness...being suspended in a vast void between heaven and earth....I felt suspended between heaven and earth with no trust or belief in anything or anyone, including God and myself" (Q.R.).

She was also given consolation and hope during this period of feeling lost: "the kindness of people God placed in my path, the lessons painfully learned, showed me over and over, after each storm, that God had been there through it all" (Q.R.).

The image of a path in a great forest was also used:

Sometimes the path becomes too narrow or hard to see, sometimes it is hidden by vines and branches, sometimes I wander off course farther, and sometimes I don't want to go any further, but I know the path is there and I pray that God helps me to keep putting one foot in front of the other. (Q.R.)

One night I listened intently as a group of my married friends and I gathered for reflection on midlife. I heard them speak of their old maps, of things in their marriages that worked well for a long time but had become inadequate. They spoke about parenting styles, their methods of handling finances, role changes, their means of communication, especially the need to share their feelings and not just their ideas. Their understanding of what marriage meant was also changing. They struggled for how to allow other intimate relationships into their own, when to stand up for one's own direction of growth and when to compromise. Mixed in with all this marital lostness was each one's individual lostness as well. As the old maps of marriage disintegrated, so too did their personal ones.

One of my unmarried friends also struggled with old maps. She was in her late thirties before she recognized and accepted her homosexual orientation. The "old map" of how she related sexually no longer worked. Yet, she faced tremendous fear and insecurity: would she be able to cope if she let go of the old map? Would her friends and family accept her? How honest could she be with the people in her life? Where would the new territory take her? How would it affect her work, her life with God, and her experience of religion in a church that rejected her sexuality? Well into her late forties now, she continues to wander in new territory, gradually feeling at peace and grateful for having left the old map behind her.

During midlife we may not only feel lost, we can get lost in something and lose ourselves even more. Becoming totally and compulsively absorbed can be a way of avoiding the pains of midlife growth. Giving all of one's time and energy to work, becoming "lost" in sex, exercise, food, shopping, books, sports, or any other diversion can be a source of keeping us from facing our directionless situation.

Significant midlife transitions such as bodily changes, job dissatisfaction, relational struggles, and role issues often take us to the land of "Don't Know." This place is gray with questions that have no easy answers. It is a foggy land of insecurity, confusion, and distress. Stephen Levine describes how the Korean Zen Master Seung

Sahn teaches that we must learn to trust this land of "Don't Know" because it is from here that wisdom comes forth. When we trust "Don't know" we do not cling to the past. We do not hold onto old points of view and stagnant opinions. When we trust "Don't know" we are open to being in process, with many possibilities and alternatives. We do not force things to happen. "Don't know" waits and explores, searches and considers, examines and trusts. Levine also notes that "the difference between confusion and 'don't know' is that confusion can only see one way out and that way is blocked, while 'don't know' is open to miracles and insights."[3]

Not all midlife journeyers feel negative about their searching or feeling lost. "I used to wear many hats," wrote a respondent. "Now, I just wear the hat of a seeker." She felt very good about this and appreciated the image of searching. Another respondent was also enthused at the possibility of what there was to discover:

> What makes the journey image significant for me is the sense that there is a path to discover. A journey for me is different than a trip in that there is the element of surprise. On a journey things happen that are not planned and yet are part of the plan. When I can view what is happening to me from this vantage point it helps me to cope with the uncertainties along the way.... it gives meaning to events that seem meaningless. (Q.R.)

One woman told a story of how she experienced being lost and having no maps. She had chosen to hike a hard route to a mountain peak. The rest of the group arrived ahead of her. As she had to take an extra day she was left behind with the ranger. There was no trail or map for this section of the climb. He told her to take the lead and he would follow. The ranger said that there were "no prescribed routes" but she would figure it out. At first she was terrified, but then decided to trust the ranger who she knew would look after her. This tough experience was a very liberating one for her. She felt empowered by him to find her own way through the area with no trails. After she returned home, she carried this truth over into her life which was currently full of searching (Q.R.).

Whether we are feeling lost because we need to leave something or someone behind, or need to recover a part of ourselves, or need to move into something totally new, or we are experiencing the lostness that comes in the form of an escape, our movement toward wholeness and "being found" will require waiting. Accepting the not knowing and having to wait can oftentimes be the hardest part of midlife. Nor Hall notes: "Letting things come of their own accord, or grow in their own time, often looks and feels like complete stagnation. But angels come out of those depths.... As Jung put it: a part of life was lost but the meaning has been saved."[4]

We are pilgrims who are on the way. When we come to the gateway of the second half of our life there are more questions than there are answers.[5] This dimension of questions was echoed in a respondent's insight:

> It's hard for me to describe my spiritual journey because I feel that somewhere along the way I've begun to take a different path and I don't know where it is leading me. I do feel good about my new path, but probably have many more questions than I did before. (Q.R.)

Waiting in our lostness is vital for our growth. This waiting provides the time needed for growth and for clarity. Waiting has the feel of being very passive but it is also an active thing. We choose to wait in the lost space with no maps because we know, instinctively at least, that the time is not yet right for us to find what is needed. Sue Monk Kidd uses the image of the cocoon to emphasize how significant this waiting period is. When we are lost in the seeming "nowhere" of life, there is actually much growth going on. It may feel like nothing is happening, that we are just roaming around inside, but there are very important changes going on. She warns: "If you don't show up prepared to wait, you may miss the transcendent when it happens."[6]

The image of a plant leaf slowly unfolding has helped me to accept this waiting period and the discoveries of truth that midlife offers. Unfolding can seem to be a terribly long process, especially when one is in much pain. Unfolding implies a steady yet often imperceptible growth. When something is unfolded, one sees gradually what has been covered and unknown: relationships unfold, the meaning of life unfolds, the mystery of who we are unfolds. At each step of the journey we slowly learn more about these vital aspects of our lives. Unfolding cannot be forced but it can and must be nurtured just as a plant with unfurling leaves needs to be watered and given light.

When we are experiencing inner growth, something in us yearns for instant finding instead of gradual unfolding. We want to find the way and we want it now. The Child in us stamps her feet, demanding that something happen. A part of us yells such things as: "I want to know my true Self now instead of stumbling around wondering if I am headed in the right direction. Let me know where I need to go with my life. Let me get on with what I am supposed to do so I can do it. I want this unfinishedness of mine to be done." Instant discovery is rarely the way of deep growth, however. It takes time for a seed to sprout, a leaf to unfurl, and a bud to bloom. All our worry and efforts at anxious control will not speed our inner growth.

Midlife is a time to recognize the pilgrim in us, that part of us which stumbles in confusion and wanders in the gray mist of unknowing. It is a time to grow in trust, believing that the stars that shine in our soul will lead and guide us to the future. Midlife is a time to be less concerned with being lost and more focused on waiting to be found. It is a time of profound and meaningful exploration if we allow it to be so.

Simmering Time

1. With what images of being lost and searching do you most identify? Do you have images of your own that express what it is like to be lost or without direction?

~

2. Draw a map of your life from your earliest years. Highlight all the significant events and turning points that have led you to this present time and place. Sit with the map and let it speak to you of

your life. Then deliberately place the map somewhere out of reach where you can no longer see it. On another paper begin a new map to symbolize your future. Sit with this empty, unmarked map. Allow your thoughts and feelings to come as you face uncharted territory. Think about your life now. Give this map a title.

~

3. Make a list of what seems to be lost in your life. Which of these need to be left behind and which ones need to be recovered?

~

4. Reflect on this passage of Ann Bedford Ulanov:

> Meaning does not come to us in finished form, ready-made; it must be found, created, received, constructed. We grow our way toward it. And sometimes the precious bit of true self, the unlived bit of soul, hides in psychological complexes, in illness, even in tragedy, even in sin.... Some mysterious power uses what we see as horrific and as the defeat of all our hopes to bring about our salvation.[7]

Create a mandala of your unfolding midlife journey.[8]

~

5. *Questions for journaling and/or discussion:*

- Have you ever felt lost or without direction in your midlife journey? If so, what was this like for you?

- Who or what helped you find courage to continue searching when you felt lost or directionless?

- What is unfolding in your life? Is there a particular area in which you seek meaning? What is being found, created, received, and constructed?

- How are you seeking deeper meaning?

- Is there a part of your life that is unwanted but that may be leading you to a new inner destination?

~

6. Go for a slow walk in a park, or stroll leisurely on busy city streets, or amble along a beach. Let yourself meander aimlessly for awhile. What is it like not to have to get to a certain place or destination?

~

7. Thomas Merton once wrote a prayer that began, "I have no idea where I am going...." Have you communicated with God when you've been wandering? If so, what was this communication like? Write a prayer of "the lost one."

~

A Prayer for One Who Feels Lost

As another day begins I give myself to you, God. I entrust myself into your care, believing that any struggles that come my way today will have the potential of bringing me wisdom. You have been my strength and my courage when my inner world has been bleak, dark, and dreary. Guide me now in my time of feeling lost.

Source of Light, Source of Love, I turn to you. Be the companion of the lost part of myself as I search for what is needed in my life. Deepen my yearning for you as I wander through the twists and turns of my self.

Come, be with me, Eternal Home, as I search for the road that will lead me more deeply into your heart. Take me by the hand and be the radiant Companion whose presence is enough to give my heart hope and vision. When I feel lost and forlorn, draw me to yourself. As I search for the unnamed pieces of my life, lead me home, lead me home.

—Joyce Rupp

CHAPTER FOUR

Midlife Grief: The Tolling of the Black Bell

"Life is all beginnings and ends. Nothing stays the same, lad," my granpa said at last.... "Parting, losing the thing we love the most, that's the whole business of life, that's what it's mostly about."

—BRYCE COURTENAY

a large black bell
solemnly tolls
in my soul
calling me
to the Vesper
of tears.

I enter the chapel
of my life
but the tears
pull away into themselves,
refusing to fall
on the prayer
of my heart

thus it is
that sadness reigns
quietly, intensely,
day in, day out

and the tolling
of the black bell
goes on and on

—JOYCE RUPP

I LOVED LIVING on an Iowa farm when I was young, but there were some things that brought great sorrow to my childhood heart. One of these happened every autumn. My father would buy calves from a Montana rancher so that he could feed them on rich Iowa corn throughout the winter and have them fattened for market when early summer came. These young calves, newly weaned from their mother's milk, were shipped by truck across many miles. The first week that they lived on our farm they would bawl and bawl for their mothers in Montana. It was an awful thing to hear their wailing through the nights and days. Nothing could be done except to let them cry out their loss until they finally let go and were content to be on the Iowa farm.

As I think of the losses of my midlife journey, I remember those anguished cries of young calves longing for what they left behind. Midlife has demanded a moving on and a letting go of things of the past that have kept me from being myself. It has been a time of sorting through and reviewing expectations, hopes, dreams, memories, experiences, relationships, and so much more. I've tossed some things out while others I've restored and renewed. With each letting go, I have felt the cry of the young calves.

Because some things had simply to be let go, midlife has been a time of inherent loss. I have said "goodbye" to people through death and relational changes. I have let go of unhealthy behaviors and attitudes, a youthful-looking body, familiar ways of praying, and false perceptions about myself and others. Each goodbye has been like the slow, steady tolling of a funeral bell, bidding adieu to the part of myself that had to "die."

Letting go is an experience of loss that brings with it a certain amount of grief, depending on how deep and strong the letting go is. As with all grief, I needed to give my attention to the pain and distressful emotions that accompanied my loss. One late September day, I stopped to ponder four trees that were still green on the outside but full of yellow on the inside. I saw this as the pain of autumn working from within them. I thought to myself:

> how true of my life:
> little aches, angers, concerns,
> nip at my spirit and mind;
> eventually they work their way out
> and the pain becomes evident
> in the physical changes
> of my vulnerable body
> and the spiritual changes
> of my neglected soul. (P. J.)

As I read through the many pages of my midlife journals I heard my own pains of loss again and again. There were many grief-laden emotions that accompanied my spiritual, physical, and psychological farewells. On my forty-fourth birthday I noticed some of what I was losing:

> How changed I am. No longer the great loner. Deep need for companions on my journey. I feel old these days. Not just a forty-fourth birthday or the changed face I see in the mirror. More than that. I am mourning the loss of treasures — not enough energy to love all who reach out to me, not enough time left to live all my dreams. All about me people I love are dying or are dead. Fragility. Vulnerability. (P. J.)

My journals are filled with images telling of the inner struggle that grief brings. These images helped me to identify my loss, to recognize and claim the sadness, emptiness, anger, depression, restlessness, and other emotions associated with grieving. One image was that of grain being ground under a large stone — a hard, grueling task. I saw my life at work, at prayer, very much this way — just grinding it out, enduring, getting through it. Another image of myself was that of being hip-deep in water, wading along with the going very difficult.

In another journal entry, I noted that life seemed too much to bear sometimes. I felt such deep sadness. Underneath it was tiredness caused from too much work and too much stress. I was also tired of the pain of loss. I yearned for beauty, freedom from distress and worry, nourishment, and the joy of nature.

Becoming aware of my own mortality was an issue that seemed to grow more intense with the years. My father died in my forty-third year. He fell, as May Sarton says about her own father, "like a great oak, dying in a few minutes of a heart attack."[1] His death was a sharp blow of grief, hitting me with great force. I had felt a closeness to my father most of my life, had worked with him in the fields, listened to his wisdom and his challenges, enjoyed his laughter, and respected him for the man of integrity and goodness that he was. When he died, an immense void opened up in me. For over a year this loss greatly affected my work and my personal prayer. Contained within this loss of my loved one was the reality that a parent had died. A generation was passing away. Mortal time, I suddenly knew, did indeed have limits.

The following year, when a good friend — my age — died of cancer, I became increasingly aware of my own body's vulnerability and limitations. My first liver spots appeared. I found wrinkles I never had before and my hair seemed to gray rapidly. I was traveling a lot for my work and discovering that I didn't have my "old energy level." At age forty-seven, I made a trip to Liberia and knew, for the first time, the gripping fear of dreaded diseases like malaria. I had never before been afraid for my body's health in that immediate way. My body had always seemed invincible.

As mortality and other issues surfaced for me, I continually found images that gave me courage. One of these was a weeping willow tree bending and stretching, without breaking in the wild wind. It reminded me that there was "tree" enough in me to bend without falling apart.

The following entries contain two images that challenged me to accept the harsh reality of midlife loss:

Nostalgia and goodbye stalk my heart like a hunter eager for prey. I want to hide in work, run around, be busy, but something urges me to confront the inner pursuers and see what they have to say. (P.J.)

All my days now have the flavor of goodbye in them, like vanilla penetrating all the parts of a cake. Everywhere I look, everyone I spend time with, all remind me of the day when I shall die. I try to eat life and avoid the goodbye that flavors it but I simply cannot miss the strong sense of my mortality. (P. J.)

One of the greatest midlife teachings for me was when I fell asleep at the wheel of my car, going sixty-five miles an hour on the Interstate. I woke up with my car careening toward a deep ditch. I managed to get the car back on the road, but for miles after that I kept saying to myself: "You almost died. You almost died." It was a turning point for me in accepting my own mortality. It taught me how quickly death can come, that I cannot avoid the ultimate reality of my own death, and that I need to be prepared at any time for it. It also helped me to put my life in perspective, to see that the things that I thought were so important really were not, and to take more time for what I most appreciated and valued.

When I turned fifty, I decided that I wanted to celebrate my age rather than bemoan it. I was feeling very positive about myself and my life. I wanted to welcome what was ahead. I gathered some of my women friends and asked them to join me in my "entrance into the Crone-dom." The image of the Crone, the older, wise, challenging woman, gave me hope.[2] What a fun time we had, and how supported I felt, as I walked away from my youth and into my aging.[3]

I was also intensely aware of changes within my religious community during my forties. One day when I went to visit at our motherhouse, which is filled with sisters who are retired and older, I knelt in the chapel and wept. I had looked around that morning at Mass and saw how "old" my community was. I had the image of us together as one big hospice, a place of dying people. Our community had had no new members for over ten years, and I had to face the assumption that we were entering into our own process of death.

I also experienced relationship losses. There were old wounds from the past that needed tending. There were decisions I had to make about the relationships I carried with me into midlife. As I looked over the first half of my life, I saw not only who I had become but who had been with me in my "becoming." As I grew clearer about who I was, I also grew clearer about who I wanted to have in my life. I didn't have enough energy anymore for relationships that constantly drained me and gave little in return.

In the past, I would have clung to these stale, unnourishing relationships on the pretext of "being nice" or "avoiding conflict" or "giving no matter what the cost." Instead, I risked being thought of as uncaring or "un-Christian," faced my needs and my limitations of inner energy, and chose to protect my own spirit which was sorely in need of vitality. Because being faithful and responsible to relationships was important to me, I initially felt uneasy and uncomfortable with those decisions. Hidden within this process was also a letting go of an old message of mine that said I always had to respond to other people's needs. This recognition was another loss that needed grieving.

I had also grown in a different direction from some of my friends and colleagues and found that we had less and less common ground to bond us. I deliberately withdrew from some people and chose to bid them farewell, albeit with some sorrow and guilt, not knowing if I was being selfish or making a healthy decision. I rechose other relationships and opened myself up to new ones that I firmly believed would bring me life, and did. (As I look back upon the choices I made, it seems quite clear to me now that the decisions were good ones. At the time, however, some of those choices were riddled with questions and confusion.)

Because of these many types of losses that were a part of my midlife years, it seemed like I was often walking inside of depression or around the edge of it. I ate and slept in my usual pattern, enjoyed wonderful successes in my work, discovered delightful and loving personal relationships, but there were still times when I felt blah, inept, empty, caught in some kind of midlife doldrums deep inside. This corridor of fog descended on my spirit periodically and left me full of grief:

Yesterday seemed like a slowly moving giant of sadness in me. More than that. Nothing had much meaning. Just doing. Getting through. Lost, empty, meaningless day. I need to be keenly aware of desolation at this time in my life, be aware of where it comes from but, more so, where I let it take me. (P. J.)

In spite of all the emotions of grief that churned around inside me, I always found pieces of hope in images that surprised me. Something from the earth or from a particular season would speak to me, such as the falling leaves of autumn or the way that plants gathered up energy during the winter months. I would do something so simple as pause by a small pond in the woods, seeing the reflection of barren yet beautiful winter trees as a reflection of my own pain, and I'd feel a sense of hope.

I had times of nostalgia about the past. Tears would come to my eyes as I sensed the beauty of persons or places. At other times I would long to be out of the pain of the struggle and want to run away from it, to "feel good" again the way I did before midlife moved in. I experienced this as restlessness, and at other times I felt kind of stunned by the whole thing, like one who first hears of a death:

The first rush of winter cold comes banging on my window. Morning news proclaims snow; the air tells of its coming. I feel shell-shocked. My inner life is that way, too. Don't want to admit it. Stunned. Just moving rather unfeelingly. Death movement in the outside world and in my heart as well. (P. J.)

Something in me wants to run today, to jump up and out of meditation, to be busy and active. I think that I want to avoid the reality of being here . . . deeper emptiness, loneliness, desire to be at home. Maybe a fear of what you want to say to me, God. Anyhow, I thank you for the grace to sit in my restlessness and not run. (P. J.)

I also looked at my life and what I had not done well. I had to admit my failures and let go of things that I wished I would have done differently. I had to offer myself forgiveness and welcome with trust the wiser person I was becoming:

This year I will be forty-six years old. I feel myself "getting old." I've wasted a lot of psychic energy fighting those who've been against me. I'd wish to undo this but I cannot. However, I am learning, growing wiser, and I'll try hard to not do that "fighting against" anymore. (P. J.)

One of the midlife emotions that caught me off guard was the rise of anger in me. I didn't expect it. I was basically a "calm and peaceful" person, very "nice." As I went further inside, all the anger I never allowed to come out rose up to greet me. At first I felt disjointed and ugly. I didn't want to have that anger. I realize now that this recognition of anger was a gift for me.

When I went deeper I found anger there: anger about the unjust treatment of women in the Roman Catholic Church, anger about old religious community situations in which authority was used to control and dominate, and things of my childhood that needed to be left behind. I found a deep well of sadness — about celibacy and not belonging, and about the lack of freedom and creativity where I worked. I felt the anger like raging tentacles inside of me:

> jagged fingers reach out in my soul
> one set is icy cold
> the other red hot flames,
> the hands meet, sizzle, snap,
> the fingers search
> touch inner places of my being
>
> the ice-cold tentacles
> probe, paralyze, and pain,
> the red-hot flames
> sear, suck, and suffocate
> and worst of all
> they pursue love and terrify her
>
> she hides in the tiniest recesses
> of my soul while
> I shudder at losing her

> and I go alone in my soul
> crying out for love
> to come home. (P. J.)

I came to terms with anger when I discovered two photos in a *National Geographic* magazine. One was of a fierce-looking adult lion racing through a jungle, getting ready for a kill. The other was of two lion cubs playfully pawing with one another. It was then that I saw how anger had many "faces" and that it could be a strong protector for me when I was being treated unfairly or when I needed to confront things that I'd rather avoid. I stopped feeling badly about having anger and began to sort out what anger I needed and what had to be sent on its way because it took too much energy from me.

I consistently experienced the ups and downs that are a natural part of grief. While I felt the sadness and the terror of loss, I also had times of enthusiasm and hope. I knew I was learning a lot from my midlife experiences and sensed that there was life beyond the loss. Again, I found images to help me name this dimension of grief and to console me in the midst of my pain:

> November surprised us all
> delicious warmth, balmy breath,
> trees almost barren grew confused
> and pushed new buds out on limbs
> birds gathering for a long flight
> decided to stay and sing awhile longer
>
> and I, I forgot for a moment
> that desolate midlife soul of mine
> I was content, for a moment,
> to be discontent
> to be at peace in the wasteland
>
> November surprised us all
> and even though we knew
> the cold, bare howl of winter
> was hiding over the next hill,

we sat back, smiled,
and felt delicious

it is these tiny islands of hope
in an all too desolate heart
that sustain the weary wanderer
on the path of midlife purging (P. J.)

Midlife: A Journey of Loss and Recovery

Many comments on the questionnaires reflected the "tolling of the black bell" of grief that the respondents had experienced in their midlife journey. Few directly addressed the issue of grief itself but many referred to the emotional response that grief induces. This is reflective of numerous adults who do not see transitional times as those that bring about grief. The emotions associated with grief still seem to be relegated mainly to the death of a loved one but, in reality, many of the emotions that arise during midlife are those of grief, emotions that surface due to loss and letting go.

As a respondent described her experience of midlife, I noted how she named many grief-related aspects such as "changing values, indifference, cynicism, numbness, paralysis, shattering of idols, caring deeply and withdrawing. . . ." She went on say: "Sometimes I wonder if this has been a terrifying and horrible wake-up call and I'm refusing to push the button on the alarm."

Midlife involves considerable loss. Not only is there the sense of the passing of the vitality of our youth; there is also the loss of certain aspects of self, loss of the person we thought we were. This involves letting go of how we previously viewed ourselves and what we hoped for our lives. It means letting go of the notion that something or someone else is going to fix our lives for us. Midlife offers us the awareness that we are the ones responsible for our lives. One respondent commented: "I left teaching to go to seminary to find myself. I felt like I had given myself away and I didn't know what I wanted anymore" (Q.R.).

As we lose who we thought we were, we may feel adrift on the sea of life, carried along on the sea of sorrow and sadness. It is usually at this juncture in personal growth that people begin to realize that what gave their lives purpose, direction, and enthusiasm no longer works for them. For example, their lives may have been centered on goals of getting ahead or accumulating power.[4] A midlife woman described this with the image of "getting off the ladder and joining hands with others in the circle" (Q.R.). This recognition, and the consequent choices to alter a power-over approach to life, can involve a great loss for the individual because it involves detaching one's self from something that gave energy to one's life but that now needs to "die."

Many midlife persons experience the death of one or both parents or take on the responsibility of decision-making regarding the care of an aging parent.[5] At the same time, they see their children grow into adulthood and move away from them both physically and psychologically. One respondent wrote:

> When our children grow and become independent, they have energized us so much, for so many years. When they leave, a part of us dies and leaves with them, because a stage of our lives is over, and death looms larger. (Q.R.)

The illness or death of friends and colleagues who are of the same age as we are confronts us with our own mortality. It is also during this period that we are more vulnerable to being caught in the cold web of job loss or forced into early retirement. These reminders of our own fragility and the stark truth of how short life is call us to greater appreciation of the present moment and the gift of life. This urgency to live life fully is reflected in an image that a woman offered: "Just below the timberline summer lasts only three weeks. The fragile, wild flowers bloom profusely but only for a short time. Therefore, they'd better be about celebrating summer and not just contemplating blooming" (Q.R.).

Midlife grief comes from the dying of dreams of who we hoped to be and what we longed to do with our life. Included in this is the facing of our limitations, be those physical, emotional, or psychological. We are forced to see what is and is not possible for us given our age and our life situation. Accepting these losses is an experience of inner dying, and thus mourning and grief are typical and necessary responses to these losses. Feelings of sadness and depression will be present as attachment to these things is given up.

It seems quite natural that there might be losses associated with our more intimate relationships, and yet how we fight this inevitable possibility. When we lose a sense of "who I am," our relationship with others who have known us well can also be affected. We may feel that they do not understand, listen to, or accept us, and indeed, they may not. They may be trying to keep us in the secure mold of the person we were in the first half of life. Unless others give us room to grow, we may wither and die or choose to bloom in another field.[6]

It is not surprising that there would be struggle and grief associated with midlife loss because one's security or stronghold is seemingly destroyed or taken away. One respondent used the image of roots to speak of this: "I remember taking out the front bushes by our house and the deep roots leaving a big, black, empty hole, just like all of the significant changes and losses that were occurring in my life" (Q.R.).

Another person described this loss as that of "falling into a black hole in space" (Q.R.). Another used a very different image to express this great loss in midlife. She said she felt like "a peaceful nest shaken" in which the bird became terribly frightened because it seemed like there would never be a secure home again (Q.R.).

It is difficult to let go of how we have learned to master the world. We must find a different way "home."[7] The midlife person is undergoing personal change and is leaving behind a former way of relating to the self and to the external world. This leaving behind involves mourning what is passing or past and will be no more. Grief is painful and we are tempted to think we can avoid it and all the difficult emotions that come with it, but we cannot, not if we want to become more whole persons.

This time of grieving in midlife, which is most often brought about by experiencing loss, is usually a time of darkness when many repressed feelings rise to the surface such as anger, sadness, despair, resentment, rage, blame, vengeance, betrayal, fear, shame, and guilt. A respondent used the images of "a tomb of numbness and a void of emptiness" to express this. When these feelings come forth, one must pass through them in order to come to wholeness. These very emotions are a part of the cycle of death and rebirth and are necessary elements for our personal growth.

Roger Gould writes:

> To achieve an adult sense of freedom, we must pass through periods of passivity, rage, depression, and despair as we experience the repugnance of death, the hoax of life and the evil within and around us. To enjoy full access to our innermost self, we can no longer deny the ugly, demonic side of life, which our immature mind tried to protect against by enslaving itself to false illusions that absolute safety was possible.[8]

I recall giving a retreat where almost all those present were in midlife. As they came for individual conferences I heard "loss" over and over. It was not only having to let go of some of their "old" world, but there was also fear of the "new" person they were choosing to become. They were filled with questions such as: If I change, will I be loved in this new way? Do I want this marriage to continue? Do I want to live alone the rest of my life? How can I use my talents in a new way? What do I do with all this hopelessness I am feeling? When these questions flood the midlife mind and heart, many grief-like emotions will emerge.

In spite of all this loss and grief, there is also renewed hope and promise. What has died gives rise to other valuable and welcomed gifts. May Sarton knew this at fifty-eight:

> I am proud of being fifty-eight, and still alive and kicking, in love, more creative, balanced, and potent than I have ever been. I mind certain physical deteriorations, but not *really*....Wrinkles here and there seem unimportant compared to the Gestalt of the whole person I have become in this past year.[9]

While death to one's youthfulness can seem like a tragic thing at first, gradually one comes to realize that the things of youth no longer provide the nourishment and vitality that they once did.[10] The reality of death, if approached in a healthy way, can be an introduction to a new level of consciousness. In fact, "the more a soul develops in spiritual awareness, the smaller the threat of death. Death is life's last great challenge to the ego to free the soul."[11] Facing one's death, along with all the other losses of midlife, provides the opportunity to revalue one's life and to put things in a new perspective. This allows for greater inner freedom and deeper contentment with life.

Numerous respondents suggested that certain images brought them comfort in their midlife losses and encouraged them to go on in the midst of their mourning. For one person, a lighthouse was "a beacon of hope along the journey especially in those times of loss and darkness" (Q.R.). Another told of a smooth stone that she chose at a retreat. She felt it represented how she wanted her life to be. As she was meditating on this aspect, she turned the rock over and there was a hole in it. At first she was distressed at not having a perfect stone. Then she realized that the hole represented the losses in her life of "on-the-spot motherhood, friends who moved, died of cancer, etc." She said, "As I looked at the stone, it was evident that life will always have holes but the smooth times help me get over the bad (hole) times" (Q.R.).

Whether we are facing the reality of our big Death or the many little deaths of our daily existence, we will feel these deaths more keenly when we are in the midst of our midlife journey. The healthiest way to growth is to face these losses and claim their accompanying grief. Let the midlife bell of grief ring. It not only announces our losses; it also proclaims our healing. Our grieving does not need to last forever. We will one day look back and see that these losses have faded in our memory while our wisdom and inner freedom have taken on a vibrancy that we never could have imagined.

Simmering Time

1. Which image described in this chapter most speaks to your own midlife experience of grief? Is there an image from your life that speaks more fully to this experience?

~

2. Listen to music that draws you inside. Reflect on your midlife losses, on who and what you have had to let go. Mentally gather all these into a basket (or write down these things and place them in an empty basket). Allow your spirit to feel the grief of having to say goodbye to all these things.

~

3. Look back over your midlife journey. What are the predominant feelings that have returned to you over and over? Are any of these associated with grief, such as: restlessness, confusion, sadness, increased or decreased eating/sleeping patterns, anger, despair, discouragement, numbness, loneliness, panic, guilt, resistance, resentment, backaches, headaches, stomachaches...?

When is the last time that you allowed yourself tears over some experience or event that was one of loss for you (tears of anger, sadness, discouragement...)? Talk to your tears if they are deep inside of you and are refusing to come out. If your tears easily come forth, celebrate them in some way.

~

4. *Questions for journaling and/or discussion:*

- When did you first become aware of your losses and your limitations? What was this like for you?

- How would you describe your experience of midlife grief?

- As you have experienced losses and discovered limitations of body, mind, or spirit, which one has been the most difficult for you to experience and to accept?

- Who/what has helped you to grieve your losses?

- Have you found any benefits or blessings through your encountering losses and limitations during midlife? If so, what are some of these?

~

5. Draw or paint a mandala of your experience of loss and grief in midlife or draw a black bell. Around it write words describing your midlife experience of loss and grief (emotions, events, names...).

~

6. Go for a walk in a cemetery. Let yourself feel the losses you've known in your midlife journey. Then go and purchase some flowers or a plant that is in bloom. Take this home with you and sit with this beauty as you ponder your midlife grief.

~

7. As you reflect on your midlife bereavement, how do you respond to these two questions that Sogyal Rinpoche poses?

> You can learn so much, if you let yourself, from the grief and loss of bereavement. Bereavement can force you to look at your life directly, compelling you to find a purpose in it where there may not have been one before. When suddenly you find yourself alone after the death of someone you love, it can feel as if you are being given a new life and are being asked, "What will you do with this life? And why do you wish to continue living?"
>
> —SOGYAL RINPOCHE, *The Tibetan Book of Living and Dying*

~

A PRAYER FOR
MIDLIFE GRIEVING

Compassionate One,
I sit with empty hands
wondering about the losses
of my life.

I sit with empty hands
pondering the pain
of many goodbyes.

I sit with empty hands
searching for decisions
about difficult choices.

I sit with empty hands
facing the limitations
of my aging.

I sit with empty hands
looking for my life
among the broken pieces.

I sit with empty hands
sifting through dreams
that have disintegrated.

I sit with empty hands
feeling the ache and sorrow
of all my losses.

I sit with empty hands
yearning for the unfolding
of my true identity.

Compassionate One,
I sit with empty hands
trusting that your presence
embraces my pain,
shelters my vulnerability,
and gives meaning
to my countless dyings.

—Joyce Rupp

CHAPTER FIVE

Midlife Prayer: When the Bush Doesn't Burn

This darkness and this cloud, no matter what you do, is between you and God, and hinders you, so that you can neither see God clearly... nor feel God.... Therefore, prepare to abide in this darkness as long as you must, evermore crying after God whom you love.

— The Cloud of Unknowing

my midlife yearning for God
takes me down alley ways
chases me on dark roads

I bump into brick walls
run from loneliness
get horribly distracted
follow fading fantasies
search long winding trails
only to find a dead end

but everyday I start again

rarely does it taste good
or seem to lead anywhere
but something (someone)
draws me forward
and I cannot leave
unattended
my morning place of prayer

perhaps it is
the unspoken truth
that something more
than emptiness
is taking up residence
in me

it is the whisper of Love
which holds my frailness
the soft voice of Tenderness
that warms my loneliness
the quiet breath of Life
that draws me as I die

—JOYCE RUPP

T HE COVER ON THE JOURNAL of my forty-first year of life shows a small, weatherbeaten rowboat. It sits at a slightly upward angle on a sandy piece of land far from water. It appears abandoned. Tall, wild autumn grasses of brown and rust have grown around it. The contrast is striking — what was made for slipping through the freedom of water is silent and immovable as it sits amid a season of dying. I remember how I felt about my spiritual life as I carefully chose that picture for my journal cover. Without a doubt, I was that boat — dead, drab, lifeless, waiting and waiting. God seemed nowhere to be found. I felt as though I had been moored forever and could not get into the "water" of my depths unless someone took me there. I realized that the "someone" was God.

I have often laughingly commented to my friends that I was going to write a book about midlife prayer and title it: *When the Bush Doesn't Burn.*[1] I suppose I laughed in order to take the pain off the truth of how I felt about my spiritual life. During my late thirties and forties my relationship with God felt like a constant struggle of hoping for an intense closeness but feeling distant and lifeless. Unlike Moses, who was drawn to a fiery bush in which God spoke to him, I had a bush that not only did not burn, it seemed dead and fruitless. I was unaware, except for small glimmers now and then, that my union with God had any life to it.

The overall view I had of my spiritual life was that of a great stretch of darkness and a vast area of wilderness. There was a void in me that would only momentarily be filled with an awareness of truth, light, joy, beauty. The darkness scared me and I grew concerned that I might "lose God" completely:

> Have I been afraid of the darkness after all these years? Am I afraid of my very self? My deepest Self? I know that the descent to the Self can be a perilous journey. Yet, aren't you there, God? Isn't the center, the core, a very tranquil place? (P. J.)

About five years after this, I realized that I was slowly discovering how the darkness was a blessing for my spiritual growth. It was a means of leading me into surrender. I had to give up control, feel vulnerable and helpless, and throw myself into the arms of God. I had expected that if I prayed "correctly," found the "right way" to pray, or prayed long enough or intensely enough, I'd have a regular stream of burning bush moments. I figured that the greater control I had over my spiritual life, the greater assurance I'd have of feeling good about what happened when I prayed. I discovered painfully that just the opposite was true. It was when I let go of trying to control what happened in prayer that genuine joy and peace moved in and set up residence in my soul.

I also thought that as I grew older and matured on my spiritual path I would have some very definitive signs of God's nearness. I did have these moments of communion, but they were rarely in my meditation time where I thought they *should* be and most often in some surprisingly ordinary situation where I didn't expect them to be at all.

During all the ups and downs, I never felt totally abandoned by God but I struggled greatly with who this God is, how to name or image this God, how to relate, and especially, how to pray to this God. I longed for good feelings in my meditation. I hunted for a God who was cozy and comfortable. I didn't know that I was being called into a decidedly different relationship with God until I was in my late forties. I kept clinging to the old ways. In the past, I had based my daily meditation on the Hebrew and Christian scriptures. I found great nourishment there. When midlife came along, I found that these scriptures no longer worked for my meditation. I still loved many passages and read the scriptures regularly but they got in my way when I meditated. I felt guilty, frustrated, and discouraged.

The food I received from my daily meditation tasted like the unsavory locusts of John the Baptist's nourishment in the desert (Jn 1:3–12). I ate it, but it had no appeal. In my journal, I referred to my prayer with a variety of images: "sawdust prayer — arid and desolate, an abandoned junk-yard — dry, dusty, full of clutter, spiritual confetti — disconnected, no sense of wholeness." One day when I awoke, I found a dead spider curled up under my pillow. I thought it named accurately how my life with God was. During one of these unsatisfying times I wrote:

> There's something in me that yearns and yearns and yearns and yearns for you, God, and seems so unsatisfied. My morning prayer is like going to the table with my stomach growling and eating and eating, still feeling starved when I leave the table. My taste buds are holding out for something else. Is this a new stage of my spiritual life? Is this a time when I simply need to be grateful for the yearning, when I need to be faithful to your presence? I do not know. I do not know how to commune with you anymore. (P. J.)

That was exactly what was happening — a new stage in my spiritual path was opening for me but I was denying it and fighting to keep what I had known. I couldn't imagine that the void, with its emptiness and darkness, was a move toward deeper union with God. I didn't know that I was being emptied so that I could hold more of God. I was being led into contemplative prayer, but it simply felt like a dark, frustrating experience.

Part of this "new stage" was learning how to trust my own spirituality. Since my childhood on a farm I had always felt a sense of divine presence when I was with the earth. As an adult I had grown to believe that my love of the earth and the joy and meaning I found there were secondary to the kind of prayer I had learned through my religious training. My religion was filled with warnings about heresies such as pantheism, which holds that God is everything and everything is God. However, I consistently received hope and an inner vitality from the world of nature. The majority of images that sustained me were those of the earth: early morning walks, bird songs, trees of every season, little creeks gurgling with freshly melted snow, harvest moons.

Anytime I was with the earth in a contemplative mode, I found a taste of honey for my soul. I was always grateful for what I received from being with the earth, but I kept dismissing this as a secondary source of connection with God until, late in my forties,

I saw clearly how this was the primary way I was meant to "find" the divine presence.

This strong attraction to God through nature was confirmed through a surprising experience. About four years after my desert call to go deeper, I experienced a "moon moment" that captured my entire being and convinced me that the journey inward was, indeed, taking place. It was the most profound mystical experience that I have ever known. It happened on a March morning in early dawn. I was very tired that day but managed to rise, sleepily dress, and go for my usual walk. I was trekking up one of the hills near home, my head lowered slightly due to my weariness, when I suddenly became aware of a presence with me. I looked up and stopped. Stunned, I could not move. I remember letting out a huge gasp of "Oh!" I stood there transfixed.

To this day I cannot comprehend how the moon appeared as it did. There at the top of the hill I saw a complete full moon, absolutely stunning. This radiant globe looked as though it was touching the earth, filling up all the space at the end of the hill between the trees that lined both sides of the street. All I wanted to do at that moment was to walk and walk and walk until I walked into the heart of the moon. As I continued up the hill, mesmerized by the circle of light, I recall thinking that I wouldn't have minded at all dying at that moment if it meant being united with the powerful round light beyond me. It was a feeling of complete freedom from this life. Nothing mattered to me except the presence of the moon. This experience lingered with me for many months, always giving me courage and hope.

Another reason why I did not go to the earth more often to receive the much-needed gift of consolation and hope was my bent toward being busy and productive. Since my early thirties I had struggled with trying to find a balance between be-ing and do-ing, between contemplation and action. My journals are filled with entries centered around this struggle.

My head was usually filled with incessant chatter about my work and my body was often a mass of restlessness as I tried to pray. I continually described this restlessness as "fifty thousand little feet inside of me" and, because there was so little room inside with all the head-chatter going on, the little feet kept bumping into one another. It was a mad race, a horrible confusion in there. Of course, the reason for those little feet was that when I allowed myself to go deeper, I saw and felt things that I did not want to see and feel:

> A part of me loves the solitude. A part of me wants to run from it. It forces me inside myself too much. I am afraid of the pain in there. I want someone or something to distract me. And is it that I am no longer comfortable being alone with you, God? Perhaps. Prayer with you has been so dry, so hard, so restless. I do not have any heart feelings for you. But in my head I never doubt your love for me or my love for you. It's an estrangement time when all the hurt of a dreadfully difficult time climbs on my back and presses me to the ground. Forget the prayer and meditation. It reminds me of my aimlessness and my inability to name who I am becoming these 40-ing years. (P.J.)

I longed to feel my past spiritual dynamism, the warmth and assurance of divine energy. I yearned for a blazing fire in my spiritual bones, but the fire was more like a tiny pilot light, barely noticeable. As with pilot lights, though, it kept on burning. This persistent, faithful spark helped to ignite my ongoing call to transformation and kept me faithful to a daily attempt to communicate with God even though I was not sure how to name this God anymore.

For the first thirty-five years of my life, I enjoyed naming God as Father and Beloved. I never doubted that God was *for* me, but I also saw God as one who demanded hard things of me. I used to dread my five-day retreats, thinking that this would be the time that God would ask the impossible of me. I wanted to please this God and stay in good standing. As I grew in accepting myself as who I am, with both my strengths and weaknesses, I also grew in my understanding of God as one who loves me unconditionally. I didn't have to perform for God and I would always be welcome in this divine heart. One of my best gifts in midlife was making this move away from a demanding God to one who embraces me wholly as I am.

As I became more attuned to the injustice of patriarchy, I found it difficult to name God as "Father." I also struggled with who Jesus was. I questioned parts of the Christology that I had accepted from the past. I wondered what it meant to be "Christian." Theologians and poets led me back to Jesus and, as Marcus Borg urges, I met Jesus again for the first time.[2] I moved away from a focus on Jesus as "Savior" and "Sacrificial Lamb" and met him as Companion, Visionary, and Teacher, dimensions that revitalized my relationship with him.

My biggest change in naming God came in my discovery of God as "Sophia," the feminine wisdom of the Hebrew scriptures. Naming God in this way felt like coming home.[3] Sophia, the Greek name for Wisdom, is the one who dances at creation, who guides and directs and heals.[4] While I continue to call God "Sophia" because I need a personal connection with the Divine, I also know deep within that all my names for God are my projections of who I am, how I want and believe this God to be. More and more, I realize that God is mystery, a loving eternal consciousness, who is most aptly described as "I am who I am" (Ex 3:1–7). I feel at peace with being unable to name God fully, realizing that all that matters is that I am in a loving relationship with the One who is without a name. I can easily join Julian of Norwich in saying, "Greatly should we rejoice that God dwells in our soul—and rejoice yet more because our soul dwells in God."[5]

Another significant piece of my midlife relationship with God needs to be mentioned. One day as I was feeling a great ache of loneliness in me I had an image that made me both laugh and cry:

> ah, yes
> says my inner self
> to me:
> a visitor is coming
> for a long stay.

stock the refrigerator,
change the sheets,
turn on the porch light.

sure enough,
there at the front door
stands the last one
I want to welcome:
Loneliness.

she marches in past me
like she owns the place,
plops down in my favorite chair
and sips my wine.

who does she think she is,
this unwelcome guest,
to help herself to my life,
intrusive and unbidden?

but then, she knows
she'd never get invited by me,
so she makes the move
and I am left
to pay the painful price.

This emotion of loneliness was not as predominant as darkness or
other emotions in midlife, but when it came to visit me, it was
intense. In the worst time of my midlife journey, I imaged my
loneliness as "a bat gone sick, hanging in my soul, never leaving the
cave." In my thirties, this loneliness came mostly from sexual longing. In my mid-forties, it became more of a longing to "belong" to
someone, to have companionship with a significant other. I knew
that my loneliness was not unique to my life as a vowed celibate.
Married women shared with me their experiences of loneliness, being with partners who would not, or could not, communicate on a
deeper level. Even married people with good, loving communication told me of their deep longing for something more than what
they had with their spouse. Single women also told of their ache

to find someone with whom to share, not just their bodies, but their souls as well. In my midlife years, I had moved from being a "loner" with a "God and me" spirituality, to seeing how vital and necessary other people were in my life. I was often aware of how God was revealed to me through other people. Eventually, I came to understand that my deepest loneliness was not for human relationships and intimacy but rather a tremendous longing deep inside for God. I knew that if I were to remain celibate, God needed to be the Center and Core of my love, the One who was enough for me. I needed God to be my Home, the "final destination" of my deepest love.

I recall an experience I had that helped me "come home" to God. I was at a little lake surrounded by bullrushes. The morning was fresh and the sunlight was flickering on the water. There were eager swallows dipping close to the lake, finding their breakfast. As I stood there contemplating the scene, I felt the sweep of God in my soul. I became, for a moment, one with that little world of loveliness. I entered into the mystery of the bullrushes' heart with their vivid green swaying in the light breeze. I was inside of them, swaying too, praising the Creator. At that moment, the wall of deadness inside of me opened. I felt entered into and received the welcomed presence of God, telling me in a wordless way that I would never be alone.

Midlife Images of God and Spiritual Experience

The experience of God varies with each person, but many relationships with God take a huge tumble into confusion and emptiness in midlife. Religious beliefs go limp. The God one has known for many years becomes a stranger. The sturdy ground of faith is swept away. There can be long stretches of darkness and feelings of abandonment or disconnection with the divine presence. These midlife people wander around inside themselves wondering where to go in their relationship with God. They also wander around outside of themselves wondering if the religion they once wore will ever fit again.

Occasionally the opposite occurs. For these persons, midlife is an exciting time in their spiritual path because they are just waking up to the spiritual journey. Until midlife, they may have given little heed to the inner life. Suddenly they find that they are filled with longing for God and hungry for spiritual growth. They marvel at what unfolds for them interiorly. They feel nourished and embraced by God, eager to learn more.

Whichever direction midlife prayer flows, there is most always some significant change involved if one is attentive to the interior life. Almost every midlife respondent I interviewed noted that his or her relationship with God had changed, or was changing. At least a third of the respondents found some darkness in their midlife spirituality. Some of these used the image of "the dark night" as named by John of the Cross to describe this void and emptiness: "My spirituality has been a dark night. At times I am content to sit in the dark and wait . . . at other times, it is so dark I find myself running within — unwilling to stop and focus" (Q.R.).

A man wrote that for nine years he had "experienced the LONG dark night of the soul . . . empty silence . . . felt betrayed and abandoned" (Q.R.). Some were simply glad to be through the darkness. Others found meaning from it, such as the woman who wrote that because she had befriended the dark and recognized its "healing, recreating powers," God was most present in the dark night that she continued to experience. Another woman described her darkness as "being suspended in a vast void between heaven and earth" (Q.R.).

Dyckman and Carroll point out that prayer is bound to be affected by midlife dynamics because human experience is the starting point and the content of prayer. They reflect upon "the dark night" and see it as the essence of midlife, a time that is filled with confusion, paradox, vulnerability, and ambiguity. It is this darkness that moves one beyond what one has known and experienced of God. It is a time of giving up control.[6]

Elizabeth Johnson also notes that the experience of God is mediated chiefly through "the changing history of oneself." Experiences such as love, loneliness, illness, and death are bound to affect our relationship with God.[7] Thus, when someone in midlife feels lost and depressed or grieves what needs to be let go, this is bound to affect how he or she relates to God. It is not surprising that prayer during these times may seem like a bush that does not burn or a boat that is moored far from the waters.

Images of God have a significant effect on one's faith-life and ethical behavior. While the reshaping of one's God-image usually happens at each stage of life, the experiences of midlife can especially influence these images, causing an intense evaluation of one's God-relationship. Just as there is a movement in human growth toward more adequate images of self, so there is a movement spiritually toward more adequate images of God and toward the God beyond all images. Once a person surrenders to the mystery of God, new images can emerge that give hope and support to the interior change.[8]

I met a midlife woman who was struggling to find work after her last child left home. As she searched for how best to prepare herself for a future job she became more and more frustrated at the lack of success she was having. Nothing seemed to fit for her. Instead of letting herself feel lost and being patient with the long process of eventual discovery, she began focusing on having to have a "sign" from God that a certain direction would be the right one for her. When this "sign" didn't come, she felt God had abandoned her and began screaming at God because she felt she'd been let down. The turning point came for her when she began to see God, not as a magical answer person pointing the way, but rather as a compassionate presence urging her to trust her talents and her life experiences. This changing image of God influenced her greatly as she grew more peaceful inside, approaching her job hunt with greater confidence.

Images abound as midlife people speak of their relationship with God. A woman who practices Native American spirituality mentioned a feather as her key image. She described how the feather came from a creation myth that promises that whenever two-legged creatures are on their spiritual path, following their passion, they will find a feather in their path (Q.R.).[9]

A number of respondents related to images that emphasize the paradox of individual uniqueness and the accompanying bondedness with others to describe their midlife spirituality. One used the image of "the cosmos" with the many stars ("Each has its own beauty and importance and...is intrinsically important to the whole") to talk of herself and of the infinite proportions of God, while another used the word "expansiveness" to describe her oneness with all the universe (Q.R.).

This sense of oneness with all of life is one of the natural developments of midlife spirituality. Midlife prayer can help develop an inner relatedness to all things. As we let go and surrender to God, an awareness of a "more than me, a beyond all this" develops.[10] This oneness does not eliminate midlife loneliness, however. Hopkins and Anderson interviewed numerous women in the United States and found that loneliness was something that many of them had experienced.[11] A midlife respondent wrote that her midlife relationship with God was like a deep, unnamed longing for a way to be and a place to belong that one knows is meant to be but often feels is far away.

A married respondent noted that her most significant image of her midlife process was that of "home." She first spoke of loneliness in relation to marriage and noted that it was "a shock to discover that even in a good and deeply committed relationship one can still be terribly lonely." She had experienced what she described as "a homesickness for God," a spiritual longing that often created a deep loneliness within herself. The image of home provided much hope for her:

> This image of the journey toward home and all that goes with it is not a negative image for me. It makes the loneliness, the uncertainty, the adventure, the exhaustion, the struggle, the continuing to put one foot in front of the other, more understandable...I have no sense of this as some heavenly after-death image but of a kind of daily and hourly homecoming that I find and then lose again. I am learning to "let go" and trust the journey more and more. (Q.R.)

Raymond Studzinski writes: "The God who is discovered in the darkness is the one who alone can meet the deep loneliness of the human heart."[12] It is God who can "cure" the homesickness of the heart that some midlife persons experience. The lonely and dark times of prayer can help us to surrender to this God for whom our hearts ache. Through this time of emptiness and going deeper, we can grow into loving, compassionate people who walk with others in a knowing way.

Coming Home to God is also coming Home to our truest, deepest selves. Loneliness can gift us by drawing us into an emptiness in which we eliminate some of the clutter that we've allowed to pile up inside us. It can pursue us and not let us anchor down in the small, satisfied, smug, secure lives to which we cling. The more interiorly uncluttered and peaceful we become, the more we know our Home that is God.

Loneliness seeds many good things in us, just as the time of the bush-without-fire does. The bush not burning is really an illusion. The midlife bush may appear not to be burning, but the roots are alive and deep. Anderson and Hopkins assure us: "Although we do not always know the way to God...God knows the way to us."[13] God will spark the fire in the bush when it is time. God will push the little anchored boat back into the waters. Midlife is a time to trust this process.

Simmering Time

1. With what images in this chapter do you most identify? Do you have images of your own that express your relationship with God during your midlife journey?

~

2. Begin with your earliest memory of when you had a connection with God, e.g., When did you first sense God's presence? Did anyone speak of God to you? What is your earliest understanding of God? How did you image God at each decade of your life? What life experiences and events influenced your relationship with God during these various stages of your life? How do you relate to God

now? Write a dialogue with God. Allow God to speak to you about your midlife experience of spirituality.

~

3. *Questions for journaling and/or discussion:*

- How would you describe your midlife relationship with God?

- Has midlife affected your understanding and your experience of religion? Have your spiritual practices changed due to your midlife journey?

- Have you experienced loneliness on your spiritual path? If so, how have you known this?

- For what do you most long in your relationship with God?

~

4. Create a mandala of your relationship with the divine presence. You may want to begin with walking or sitting meditation, or chanting in order to quiet and center yourself.

~

5. Quietly whisper the word "home" to yourself. Do this for several minutes. Note what feelings, images, and thoughts arise within you as you repeat the word "home." What does this word say to you about your spiritual path?

~

6. Does the following passage from Etty Hillesum's diary speak to you about your midlife experience of God and prayer? What would a "fruitful loneliness" be for you?

> Life may be brimming over with experiences, but somewhere, deep inside, all of us carry a vast and fruitful loneliness wherever we go. And sometimes the most important thing in a whole day is the rest we take between two short breaths, or the turning inwards in prayer for five short minutes. (Etty Hillesum)[14]

~

7. Use clay or paints or music or dance to express your relationship with God during your midlife journey.

A Prayer of God-longing

the exodus in me is marching again
and I fear the nearness of slavery.
I yearn for some unnamed freedom
and the quiet assurance of promised land.

the days stretch into sand and barrenness.
I do not taste the manna or see the cloud,
the tiny path of my faltering footsteps
tells the tale of a long, lonely journey.

are you near, God-who-never-abandons?
in my weakness, I can barely whisper your name,
in my weariness, my hand does not outstretch,
will you come, God-who-never-fails?

the exodus in me is marching again
and I am caught in struggle and pain,
fighting the demon of discouragement
who tags along and haunts my heart.

God of the wandering ones and my God
protect me from the Egypt of my own making.
Pillar of Fire and Cloud of Light,
assure me that I am not alone.

—Joyce Rupp

CHAPTER SIX

Midlife Transformation: Shedding the Skin

Letting go was mid-life's central gesture. You let go of people and you let go of expectations, and if you were lucky, you found a way to do it without letting go of hope.
                                                —ELIZABETH KAYE

she found the skin
lying there
on her front doorstep.

she told me this
in a disgusted voice,
filled with a bit of fear,
said she got the broom
and hastily swept
the skin away.

an unsuspecting snake
slipping out of
a piece of its life,
shedding a shell
of what used to be,
leaving behind
a thin transparent slip
of a former reality.

I thought:
I'd have received that skin
on my doorstep,
a graced moment of calling.
I'd have wondered
at the synchronicity
of its presence.

but then I recalled
the turns and tumbles
of my inner life,
and knew that I, too,
have swept many a skin
away from my doorstep
with just as much disgust
and terror.

—JOYCE RUPP

I ALWAYS FEEL called into the mysterious experience of transformation as I join with other dancers in the "snake dance." This dance is done in memory of Inanna, the Sumerian goddess, whose story is filled with death and rebirth.[1] The dance begins by joining hands with other dancers, circling, and chanting. The part that invites and intrigues me is the movement when each dancer stands alone and reaches down with both hands on the left side of the body, stretching low to the earth, then turns in a spiral fashion toward the right, up to the sky. This spiraling, which is done four times — to the North, South, East, and West, is meant to be the movement of a snake shedding its skin. It symbolizes the universal truth of life's transformation: all change involves some skin-shedding. When I participate in the skin-shedding dance, I feel absorbed in the truth of transformation. I see how all-encompassing and demanding it is: the old protective skin falling off so there is room to grow and the vulnerability as new skin develops.

Transformation is a process of death and rebirth. Change is a prerequisite for growth. It involves a "dying" of some sort if new life is going to burst forth. Sometimes I've felt this changing as a radical, painful stripping away, and at other times I've welcomed it like a silent snake slipping out of an old skin that no longer fits. Either way, it has demanded some dying to who I have been and some letting go of what I have known. I now realize that my transformation is an ongoing process. Always there is more skin shedding to do, but in midlife the skins seem to pile up in a hurry on the front doorstep.

So many skins have fallen off of "me" in my midlife journey. My "skins" have included old messages and assumptions about life that developed in my childhood, behaviors that bound me to unhealthy ways of approaching life, religious beliefs that kept my spiritual world too small, and boxed-in views of my self-identity. Skin-shedding has been a time of discovering what keeps me from growing. I have pursued truth, albeit unwillingly at times, and have discovered both treasures and trash in my life. Whenever I have shed any of these skins of mine, I have found freedom and truth.

These discoveries have made the transformation process worth the risk and the struggle.

All sorts of fears usually enter into my skin-shedding: fear of the pain that goes with dying, fear of the unknown something that is being birthed, fear of the emotions that might arise, fear of depression, fear of others' criticism or judgments, fear of vulnerability, fear of the length of time it might take for the death/rebirth to occur. These fears can keep me from entering into the transformative process. Kathleen Norris writes: "Fear is not a bad place to start a spiritual journey. If you know what makes you afraid, you can see more clearly that the way out is through the fear."[2] When I name my fears, I can usually surrender to the struggle that is happening.

I've had numerous dreams that called me out of my fear and into courage. One in particular had a profound effect on my growth. At a point in midlife when I was facing the option of choosing some new theories and untried behavior, I dreamed that I was in a social situation where there was a large table full of food. This table stretched across the entire room. It held a bounty of colorful, peculiar-looking, unknown foods. I stood among all the strangers who were in the room ignoring me and I wondered what food I might choose at the table that would be "safe." The only thing there that I recognized was egg salad, so I put a large helping of this on my plate and walked away from the table. When I woke up, I laughed. There are few foods that I dislike, but egg salad is one of them. Yet, in my dream, I chose the egg salad, which was a "safe" food because I knew it. How loudly this spoke to my fear of insecurity and of risking some new nourishment for myself. I resolved that day to let go of my "egg salad" approach to life.

The skin-shedding process of transformation in midlife has called me to look at what I believe to be truth, to step into the pain of my disillusionments and fading dreams, to see how my ego attempts to rule me and keep me in bondage so that I am not open to the revelation that my unconscious yearns to share. Skin-shedding has brought me the task of evaluating my persona (the "faces" I show to the world) and discerning which of these, if any, needs to be cast off. Skin-shedding has led me to peer into my Shadow and to discover treasures of my Self as well as those parts that I would rather not own.[3] Letting go of old skins has also drawn me to see my limitations, my weaknesses, and my sin.

In my early thirties, I was overcome with what I considered to be my sinfulness. A big part of this was due to the emphasis in the Roman Catholic Church and in religious life on perfectionism. While I needed to learn and accept the part of me that was capable of sin, I also needed to acknowledge that much of what I thought to be sin was not so at all. This "sin" was actually the pieces of myself that I wanted to spurn or reject, those unmanageable things that were a part of being human — unwanted emotions and personality traits. I wanted to "be perfect" but I had to come to terms and be at peace with my clay feet instead:

> Yesterday afternoon as I listened to Handel's music, I imaged myself dancing before you, God. Suddenly I was aware of how poor I am — my clothes were all torn and dirty — but then, I looked into your face and I immediately knew it was okay — that I was totally accepted by you as I was at that moment. So I danced before you, wonderfully, and then you came and took my hand and we danced together. (P. J.)

When I acknowledged and accepted pieces of my Shadow that I had rejected (tenacious, stubborn, strong-willed, tough, determined) I saw that these very things were also some of my treasures. They had helped me to have courage and to survive some difficult life situations. They had also helped me to be steadfast in my love and care. They blessed me with much needed resiliency.

I continued looking for "a giant key" to unlock my inside door, to reveal other hidden treasures, but most of all, to let me into the secret area where I could find the answers to my life's creative tensions. As I did this, I discovered and claimed some of the unwanted parts of my Shadow as well as some of the desirable aspects such as my intuition and instinctual nature, playfulness, joy, and childlike wonder.

Acceptance of the golden piece of playfulness took awhile. I was caught up in work and productivity. There is nothing wrong with work and success, but I felt pushed and shoved around by it, so much so that I didn't know how to play anymore. Numerous times I identified with the person in the Christian scriptures who is "possessed" and lives among the tombs.[4] My crazy busyness, with the obsessive pressure of "so much to do," often felt like this insane person.

I wanted some sort of miraculous inner vision like that of the person in the tombs. I wanted a deep seeing that would free me of that tomb-state in me regarding my craziness of work. I started talking to the "voice" in me that always said, "Hurry!" but it took me five years to slow down. During that time, I did a lot of reading and reflection. From this, I realized that I needed to look at the powerful hold that the "negative animus" had on my life.[5] My animus (my inner masculine) had, indeed, tried "to over-run and suppress the feminine principle in me."[6] My negative animus took over in these ways: needing to be right, believing that I had to be rational, logical, and independent, distrusting my intuition, and ignoring my feelings. I had strong opinions and was always into *doing* and frantic busyness. I was organized, well-scheduled, and responsible. I longed for a more contemplative approach to life but I constantly chose *do-ing* over *be-ing*. Do-ing was safer and kept me from acknowledging my feelings and my vulnerability.[7]

I learned my busyness from my Western culture, my German heritage, my farmer-father, from the Roman Catholic Church, and from my religious community. They all said basically the same thing: use your gifts, give generously of yourself, work, work, work, don't fail, be successful. I can still hear my father's voice when, as children, we didn't do our chores: "What are you good for?" and "If anyone around here wants to eat, they have to work." Again, images helped me to identify both the experiences and my feelings. An image of a wild river gave expression to my frustration and stress. The river was wild and strong and I was caught in the current, struggling to hang on. It was a joyless trip full of work, an unending journey that could never find a destination.

Sometimes coming to truth felt like chewing into something hard and tough that had been there for a long time. I was never sure, at first, what it was but it felt somewhat like a new tooth pushing its way to the surface. I could feel it and it was often irritating or painful but I couldn't hurry its growth. I had to wait for it to push its way out.

As much as I wanted truth, I also resisted. When I felt a stretching to new beliefs, I found myself backing off or hoping to ignore the tension. This experience felt "like a rubber band, all stretched out at one moment, ready to break. Then, the next, all shoved together unable to breathe, a back and forth thing, either too taut or else too cramped" (P.J.). Always I needed the balance of being compassionate toward myself but also not fleeing from what would bring me necessary growth.

The transformative process of sloughing off the false Self and claiming the true Self has seemed, at times, like a wrestling match or a battle:

> There's a wildness howling outside and a lot of wild things howling inside, too. Needing and yearning to be tamed. Something in me wants to keep on running. Something in me wants to be stilled. Part of me feels loved by God. Part of me feels abandoned. (P.J.)

The inner battle has been filled with contrasts or "sides": good times and lonely times and times that seemed eternally empty. There were times of tear-full beauty. There were times of tension and stress and times of profound union with God. One day in early April, I saw my midlife battle reflected in rain and snow. It seemed to me that they were arguing, pelting each other with their coldness. Snow threatened to take over the talk but rain had warm air on her side and held her own in the battle. The two, rain and snow, twirled and tumbled, a driving force in each of their voices as they fell to the ground in fury. This was typical of the driving forces within me as I searched for truth and sometimes did not like what I found.

I felt a particular ongoing battle with my ego. I could see how I let my ego push me around, shove me into work, and thrust me into an unhealthy bent toward productivity and intense success-orientation until I felt so pressured I could hardly stand it. Sometimes my true Self strongly confronted me and challenged me about this:

> Do you know what time with me would mean for you? You would feel free. You would discover beauty beyond what you've ever imagined. You would not fret and stew over your own selfish compulsions and needs and wants. You would be a wise woman. Now you are only a carrier of the trinkets of the ego. They melt like sherbet in a summer's sun. Let go before it is too late and you are so ego-absorbed that you do not hear my voice calling to you. Stop! You cannot go on this way. You were born to grow deep. You cannot do it, satisfying your ego always. Let go. Risk failure and misunderstanding. Let me be your guide and friend. I love you. (P.J.)

This battle with the ego lasted about ten years. It was a constant struggle to let go of some of the security of what I thought I knew for the vulnerability of the unknown.

Some writers use the terms "transformation" and "conversion" interchangeably, both describing the process of growth. I view conversion as *a piece* of transformation, a process that leads to greater transformation. It has to do with the changing of my heart, befriending what will always be a part of me — my personal limitations and weaknesses — and casting aside what is avoidable: my unhealthy attitudes and behaviors and my choices and decisions for non-good. Countless images related to conversion have spoken to me in my personal journals:

- A huge, hard boulder inside of me, blocking goodness.

- Looking out the window at the brittle, dead branches of winter trees and sensing the brittleness within myself.

- A thorn branch I found in one of my desolate walks when I was working with Shadow material I did not want.

- The discordant cawing of crows that sounded like my false self being judgmental and hateful.

- Ice sliding into a spring river — the hardness in me being willing to soften.

- The walls I put up that kept others out: those who begged my understanding, who needed my forgiveness, who could have grown had I been humble, who would have laughed if I had shared my joy.

- The black, dead trees of a lake that stood in the water, sticking up, poking at me, speaking of the clumps of deadness in my heart.

- Myself as a beggar, poor and empty.

- A rock covering a moist patch of ground, keeping the seeds beneath it from growing.

- A piece of wood in a fast river current being taken for a ride like a small piece of weakness tugged from my heart.

- The weeds in a garden with their deep, tough roots: some could be pulled out, others kept coming back.

- A fresh snowfall contrasted with the bleak grime that I felt inside.

I have also found images of conversion in my dreams. One night I dreamed that I stood by a small pond on a lonely farm. I carefully wrote down all my weaknesses on the many dead leaves that were piled at the water's edge. I tossed them, each leaf, each worded weakness, into the quiet water, but the leaves kept coming back to me. No current or stream would sweep them into an unknown waterway. And so it was with my life. My weaknesses kept returning to haunt me, no matter how often I tossed them away. This was a turning point for me. I had wanted to weed out all of the "bad stuff" from my life. I began accepting the truth that I would always have weaknesses and limitations. I would always have a part of myself that had the potential for all the evil of the world. It was a call to accept myself as I am and to see these parts of myself as my "teachers." It was also a call to accept the flawed condition of others.

Every touch of truth has taken me to where my true Self lives. All of these images and experiences have helped me to continue in the process of transformation and to allow the skins to fall off when the time was ripe. In my twenties I thought I could do little wrong. In my thirties I woke up to all of my flaws and was greatly dismayed. In my forties, I began to sort out what I wanted to keep and what I needed to toss away, realizing that some of those flaws would be with me forever. As I move into my fifties and beyond, I am growing into the wisdom of accepting myself as I am with my goodness and with my weakness, knowing that the process of transformation goes on and on. I can be at home with who I am and be more gentle with others because I have become more gentle with myself.

Midlife Transformation

Discovery of one's true Self and willingness to pay the price for it are key concepts in the writings of many authors of inner transformation. May Sarton insists that if one goes "deep enough ... there is a bedrock of truth, however hard."[8] Being open to new realities, giving up false assumptions, letting go of old ways of looking at life — all of these must be dealt with during midlife. We must be willing really to change and not just "switch positions" when we are aiming for truth.[9] The skin must be shed. The life we knew and the person we thought we were must be examined, evaluated, and adapted to the path that lies ahead. Power, control, security, and all the things to which we cling, must be held out and examined. It is not easy but it is essential if we are to grow.

Carl Jung termed the process of uniting the opposites within us as "individuation." It is the means by which we become our true or authentic selves. During the first half of our life we developed one portion of who we are. Midlife challenges us to discover and to own the other side, or other aspects, of who we are. Individuation involves transformation because it can be a complete turnabout, a deep change, a looking at ourselves in a very new way.[10] As one male respondent noted, this process can feel like "an upset fruit basket" (Q.R.). Another wrote:

> It is a matter of moving from continually and harshly judging myself as not good enough or doing enough and making or masking myself to be other than who I am, experiencing all the violence of that process, to loving myself as I am with mercy, kindness and nonharming, gentling ways. (Q.R.)

It is easy to deceive ourselves in order to be shielded from pain when we are faced with transformation. Truth must be our goal, no matter where it leads us. The ego can feel dreadfully insecure as the skin comes off. The ego says, "I'm scared. I might get hurt. What will others think of me? I'll lose control. I won't have any security. This was a dumb idea. I'll never be able to do this. What will so and so think?" This voice in us can be very loud, but it can also be very subtle and we may miss how strongly it is trying to divert us from our transformation process.

One way the ego can do this is by having us think our avoidance of skin-shedding is good because we are trying to avoid upsetting others. Those who are significant in our lives may be highly uncomfortable with our "new Self" when we shed our skins. They may fight, criticize, or cajole us to put the old skin back on again. This resistance of spouses, relatives, colleagues, or friends to our midlife changing gives us "a good excuse" to avoid, delay, or stop the skin-shedding that is in process. (We do need to be careful with our skin-shedding decisions in order not to deliberately bring harm to others. True skin-shedding always takes us deeper and helps us become more compassionate beings.)

Because there can be such bold (or subtle) resistances to skin-shedding, painful or traumatic events and experiences often happen that force us to evaluate our lives and to let go of the old skin. A relationship fails, a job is lost, an illness develops, someone or something significant to us dies, or a myriad of other unwanted transitions can toss us into skin-shedding whether we want it or not.[11]

It is no wonder that it might feel like there's a battle going on within us. One respondent wrote of having "recurring dreams around the battle theme...being beaten up but someone stopping the pain. My psyche is in conflict. I sometimes wake up feeling beat up. Other times I wake up in a 'changed state,' my new person feeling open and accepting, in harmony with God and the world" (Q.R.).

Midlife is the time to take a deeper look, not just an external view, but one that allows us the freedom to bump against the flaws of our own personality. This deeper looking can be highly uncomfortable because it often leaves us feeling exposed. If we do not do this deeper examination, however, the second half of life can be dull and stagnant.[12] There are illusory parts of ourselves that we love too much to shed. Yet, these parts especially have to "go" in midlife if we are to become our true Selves.

Shedding the false Self means letting go of the part of us that is not real or is not who we truly are. A respondent had a dream in which "plastic" was a key image for this false self. He interpreted the plastic as "representing the part that will not work in my future, the part that needs to be thrown away and let go of" (Q.R.). This false Self might be anything that has kept us from being who we truly are — such as an overemphasis on either the masculine or the feminine, an imbalance of extroversion or introversion, too strong a hold on externals, a driving desire or ambition that takes all our energy, a debilitating fear, a lack of self-esteem, an unhealthy dependency.

This "stripping" of the false self is a key image in the myth of Inanna. I think of this myth as central to midlife transformation. The account of Inanna, the Sumerian goddess, was recorded around 3500 B.C.E. and is thought to be the earliest recorded story of death and rebirth. Inanna is Queen of the Upperworld, or Queen of Heaven. She has much power in her dominion and uses it well. One day she decides to visit the dark underworld where she has never traveled before. What she either does not know, or has failed to remember, is that when one goes to the underworld there are seven gates through which one has to pass.

As Inanna goes through each of these gates she is required to strip herself of something that she wears, each item being symbolic of her power as Queen of the Upperworld. By the time she passes through the seventh gate and enters into the underworld, she is completely stripped. She goes naked into the unknown darkness where she dies and is reborn.

In midlife we, too, are invited to make that deep and long descent to the dark world of the unknown. If we agree to this journey, we will also be stripped of what gave us security and power. We will experience our own "nakedness" as we let go of our strong attachments, as we wonder who we are and what we are to do with the rest of our life. We too will be "reborn" as we claim the revealed dimensions of who we truly are.

Again and again, respondents described this process of skin-shedding, of Shadow-finding, of being stripped, of discovering and owning one's true Self. A respondent wrote: "I was appalled!...I found myself acting like my father — whom I disliked because of his behavior" (Q.R.). Another described this experience as feeling like he was on a stage and God was drawing the curtains to expose the beauty of who he was. God was also sitting in the seats "enjoying" what was happening. This man commented that he had the choice whether to remain on the stage or not. He could "exit stage right" if he wanted to but he didn't because he wanted to have the *courage* to face the reality of being exposed, especially in front of the mirror of himself (Q.R.).

A woman depicted this stripping process as "seeing myself for the first time and growing compassionately in love with who I am and all my personality quirks" (Q.R.). Another wrote: "Midlife is the time for living my truth, following the path of my heart, recognizing that I am doing the best I can and that is enough. It is the time to accept that other people are doing the same thing" (Q.R.).

There are many assumptions we have made that have ruled our lives. All of these need to be examined. One respondent wrote that her midlife experience of being stripped involved an experience of her "fantasies of till death do we part" being shattered. She struggled with deep feelings of rejection and a sense of worthlessness and finally discovered her own goodness and strength. As she reflected on her painful process of shedding the skin, she commented: "I no longer know the woman I was at forty-five. We don't keep in touch" (Q.R.).

This letting go of what has named us and given us direction is no easy thing. I think of the story of Sarah in the Book of Genesis (18:1–15; 21:1–7). Sarah is a strong symbol of the part of us that has gotten secure and settled. Suddenly her life gets terribly messy — she hears an inner call to pack up and head into unknown territory. It is the call of skin-shedding. She also hears that she has within her a source of new life. At first, all this seems so incredible that she simply laughs at the thought of it. Eventually, she does indeed set out and leaves her old life behind her.

Sarah's transition is often ignored alongside the call of Abraham's, but, in reality, I think hers was equally difficult. Sarah, pregnant late in life, goes into dangerous, unmarked territory with the promise of a new generation in her womb. She risks the future because she believes in the call to uproot, to shed the skin, to leave behind the only life she has ever known for the sake of a promise heard deep within herself. In midlife, we also have the promise of new life within us if only we let go of some of the well-worn securities that bind us to the past. The midlife journey of transformation takes an enormous amount of trust in the Voice that urges us to shed the skin.

Simmering Time

1. With what image of transformation in this chapter do you most identify? What does it say to you about your own life experiences? Do you have images of your own that speak to your experience of transformation?

~

2. What skins have you shed? Draw or paint a snakeskin for each major changing of yourself. Label the snakeskin with the idea, attitude, assumption, behavior, etc. that you have shed.

~

3. A bridge has long been a symbol of a crossing over, a leaving behind and a going forth. Use the image of a bridge to identify where you are with different aspects of your transformation process. One part of you may feel like it's just beginning to cross the bridge. Another part may feel like it's in the middle, while another might be nearing the end of the bridge and ready for a new vista. You could also ask yourself what kind of bridge you are on: a sturdy, concrete one? a busy freeway bridge? a bridge that needs a lot of repair work? a quiet rural one? a safe covered bridge? a swinging suspension bridge?

You might want to find a bridge to sit by, or walk on and over, or you could create a bridge out of clay or other materials as you ponder your experience of transformation. Let the bridge symbolize your inner process of growth.

~

4. Speak to your truest Self. Write a dialogue with your true Self or speak the dialogue by "placing" your true Self in an empty chair across from yourself. Allow your true Self to speak to you. Respond to what the true Self tells you or asks you.

~

5. How does the following quote of June Singer speak to your own understanding and experience of midlife?

> The most tragic failure of all is the failure to recognize our truest self, to hear its voice, and to allow it to guide us where we are meant to go. How easily we forget the spark that burns within us, urging us to become what we are capable of being! (June Singer)[13]

What is most difficult for you in this discovery of your true Self? How and when do you hear your true Self's voice?

~

6. *Questions for journaling and/or discussion:*

  • Does skin-shedding speak to your experience of midlife? If so, how?

  • What has been your easiest skin-shedding experience? What was shed?

- What has been your most difficult skin-shedding experience? What was shed?

- What has been most helpful for you in your times of skin-shedding? What are some of the wisdoms that you've gleaned through your skin-shedding times?

~

7. Select music that draws you to your inner space. Do a skin-shedding dance of your own creation. Begin by reflecting on your experience of transformation. Let your mind and heart enter into the changes of your life. Image the snake shedding its skin. Then begin your skin-shedding dance. Let it be a source of strength for you, encouraging you to shed whatever needs to be let go.

~

A Prayer for Skin-Shedding Times

There is a time for everything
a time for every season under heaven:
a time to be insecure and a time to have security.
a time to have strong opinions and a time to let them go.
a time to be confused and a time to have clarity.
a time to be healthy and a time to be sick.
a time to experience success and a time to know failure.
a time to be young and a time to grow old.
a time to feel at peace and a time to face conflict.
a time to have friends and a time for loneliness.
a time to be weak and a time to be strong.
a time to feel lost and a time to find the way home.
a time to shed the skin and a time to welcome a new one.

(This prayer is based on Ecclesiastes 3:1–8. You may wish to write your own skin-shedding prayer.)

CHAPTER SEVEN

Midlife Healing: What the Green Moss Told Me

In praying about my wounds I have come to believe that the reason these wounds take so long to heal is that I spend more time attacking them than trying to understand them.

—MACRINA WIEDERKEHR

the great wound
cries out
from the depths
of the midlife passage,
begging
for healing.

the green moss
waits silently,
along meandering brooks
beneath rocky cliffs
behind wet rocks
upon moist soil
around thick trees.

the green moss
knows
when my healing time
is ripe.

I walk,
eyes falling onto moss.
I see now
the messenger of healing,
the witness of endurance,
the shaman of resiliency.

I hear
the sweet song
of green moss,
wooing
my bleeding wound:

"you are still green,
you are alive, alive,
you have endured,
trust the power within.
it is there,
it is there."

and somewhere deep inside,
the wound I have worn
for so long
hears the song
of the green moss

and turns toward healing.

—Joyce Rupp

WHAT WAS IT, I wondered, that so attracted and drew me to Betty LaDuke's *African Healer?* I didn't know, but in my forty-seventh year, I ordered the bright colored print and loved it. The eight stars that dance across her chest had first attracted me to this art piece. The earthy African Healer sits in a birthing posture. On her red and orange dress are happy looking creatures: a turtle, a snake, an iguana, and a bird. A long stream of green ivy threads its way around the animals. The crescent moon rests on her head of three faces (maiden, mother, crone), the sun is beneath her, and an eye rests in the center of the palm of her right hand, which is raised in the air.[1]

I found myself using this image for my meditation. I would visualize the eye in the healing hand touching "the third eye," the center of my forehead. I just let it rest quietly there. That was the place where it seemed to be most needed. I wasn't fully aware yet that some of my greatest wounding was in the way I *thought about* my spirituality even though strong glimmers of this had been revealed all through my midlife years.

I also did not know what I was "praying for" two years later when I started my weekly hikes in the Colorado Rockies. I only knew that the first time, and each time thereafter, I would begin my hike with three words: "Please heal me." It felt strange to pray this as I didn't feel like a terribly wounded creature. I wasn't depressed, in crisis, or struggling with any major issues, but the words were there, so I named them. I intuited that the energy of the earth was holding a gift for me and I needed to be open to receive it. Something unmended in me needed attention.

Toward the end of my first year of hiking, I was at a workshop on "Healing Images." We did a guided imagery exercise in which we were to go somewhere that felt like a "healing place" for us and find an image of healing. I mentally went to a hilly pine forest that overlooks the ocean south of San Francisco. I thought that the trees or the ocean would be my image of healing. To my surprise, I visualized a patch of green moss. I was deeply attracted to the green and softness of the moss, but I did not understand why. Moss had never been significant to me.

After the exercise, we were invited to share our image with someone. It was no coincidence that a man from an Ojibway tribe in northern Canada was sitting beside me. When I told him about my green moss, his face lit up and his words filled with excitement. He told me that moss was a special healing object for the Ojibways, that it had been used to put on wounds because it was absorbent and clean. It had also been used for menstruation pads and for diapering babies. He emphasized that I had been given a very special gift in seeing that image.

Soon after this workshop, deep-green moss became my companion on my hikes. I saw it everywhere. I would stop and feel the moss, marvel at its constant deep greenness, study the star patterns of its wee flowers, and sense a connection with healing that I simply could not name. This continued as I walked with moss through the four seasons, always seeing a slip of its green presence by some creek, or hillside stone, even under winter's heavy coat of snow.

It was on one of these winter days when I was hiking, kneeling to lay my hand on some moss, that the message came: the green moss endures through all kinds of weather — dryness, strong sun, cold winds. I too have this enduring tenacity within me. I have survived through all the pains and struggles of midlife and have grown significantly. I too am "green." Several days later, I read one definition for "endurance": "to harden, to make sturdy, to make robust, to strengthen. . . . Endurance isn't just hanging on or putting up with something without cessation."[2] I felt a tremendous hope as I knelt there with my hand on the moss. It was as if each time I saw the moss, I was being healed because of the hope that was mirrored in my heart. *I* was the moss growing on the rock. I had endured even though my thinking about my spirituality had been off balance for a long time.

Recovery from old wounds can be a lengthy process. Usually healing happens slowly, in bits and pieces. One day we see clearly what is needed for our healing and the next day it's all foggy, blurred and hidden from view, forgotten for a time. This continues until one day we can no longer forget. The healing is too strong to ever let the truth be blurred again. This has been true for me. The African Healer and my discovery of the moss brought me the clarity I needed for being healed.

Ten years before the green moss entered into my imaging, I had a powerful dream. I thought I had learned my lessons about my spirituality then. In the dream, I was looking in the mirror. I was aghast — I saw this huge slash in the center of my forehead, from top to bottom. It was split wide open and very deep. There was no blood but I grew sick, almost gagged as I saw it. I tried to press it shut but it kept coming open. I couldn't force it to stay and I didn't want to go get stitches. Finally, I figured a way to use my forehead muscles so the wound would stay together. Then I awoke.

As I worked with the dream, I wondered what the great gaping wound was in me that needed attending or healing or to be put together. What was it that I kept avoiding or thought would simply heal itself? And what sort of wound did it symbolize? As I continued to reflect on the dream I recognized several significant messages. I couldn't take care of the wound by myself. It needed someone to put stitches in so it would heal properly. The independence of my ego needed to have the balance of the vulnerable, dependent part of my Shadow. As for the wound itself, it was in my head — my thinking was askew someplace. It was also in the place of the "third eye," the center of spiritual vision.

Two days later I went away to the woods for several days. It was there that my deepest spiritual wound revealed itself to me:

In my meditation I saw the wound again. I could not see it healed. It was a terrible ache. The image of the autumn beauty of dusk as I stood looking out the cottage window the day before came back to me. I remember when I stood there that something in me yearned to stay and stay, to ponder, to contemplate. As I pictured myself at the window, tears from deep inside welled up, the kind of tears I know whenever I am deeply touched by Beauty. And then it came together for me, why this dream of the great wounding. The wound is my unfaithfulness to my need for the beauty of the earth. This wound is the part of me that cries out to touch, to see, to be with the earth. What makes me sure of this naming of my wound is that as soon as I go to "the cottage window" in my mind, the wound disappears and I feel the greatest peace inside of me. It is a wonderful grace. (P.J.)

I knew, long before the dream, that my love for the earth was strong and deep, that I sensed the presence of God there. Yet, I failed to spend sufficient time with the earth because I was terribly caught up in the work ethic and productivity. I also doubted if being with the earth was really "prayer." I was caught in a lot of old "shoulds" about my spirituality. My religion, and the voice of spiritual authorities within it, seemed to say that my prayer and major spiritual impetus should especially be with the scriptures, with the Eucharist, and with my relationships. While I did have a sense of God and an occasional revelation of the inner journey in those places, none was ever comparable to the immanent, intense, mystical experiences I had when I spent contemplative time with the earth. It is there, more than any other source or situation, that the space between the divine presence and my own meets and is entwined, perhaps only for a heartbeat, but that moment is full of teaching and rich with consolation.

I learn and I forget, I learn and I forget. . . . That dream had a powerful effect on me, but soon after it I got caught in the pressure of work, thus losing the power of the impact of the dream. It was not until the green-moss companionship that I fully grasped and accepted the reality of the earth being my central way to God. The green moss seems to have been the turning point for me. I have a settledness within me now about my spirituality of the earth. I do not doubt it anymore. I have also confronted my false thinking and the reasons behind my need to work so hard. The healing of my great wound is having a deep effect on me.

Besides this great spiritual wound of mine there have been, of course, those myriad wounds that come with the territory of midlife. I have known some of the wounds that other midlife persons have described: childhood hurts, disenchantments, old failures and dashed dreams, self-image struggles and emerging Shadow material, relationship difficulties and endings, and great wounds that bleed in the soul but refuse to be healed until the time is ripe.

Many images have sustained, comforted, and encouraged me as my wounds have been healed. These images have been my teachers and my guides toward healing. I have learned many things about woundedness and healing from them. These images have helped me to see how essential it is to let go of old wounds in order to be healed and to stop trying to control everything, or to figure it all out, or to make it go a certain way.

A clearing place in the woods became a reflection of the clearing place I needed inside of myself. A glance at a lone autumn leaf being carried swiftly along in a street gutter led me to see how some of my hurt was leaving, being swept away. A lone leaf hanging on a tree told me how much I was clutching on to things that needed to be let go. A gate creaking as I went through it reminded me of an inner freedom that was coming as I opened and let tough things come up through "the gate" of my unconscious. The image of barbed wire helped me to identify my lack of inner freedom:

> my wounded heart
> tightly woven round
> with barbed wire
> the iron thorns
> wounding my soft flesh
> while those who press
> against my heart
> are deeply gashed.

they move back
bleeding, wounded.

I turn my heart
over to you, God,
and you come gently
snipping the hard wire
that encircles me.
you free me.
cut me loose.
the wires fly, ping away,
as you break through them. (P. J.)

I have needed to be compassionate toward myself when I was hurting. I have also needed to offer compassion and kindness to others. One of my best sparks for love and for forgiveness of old relationship hurts came from an image of myself at the Last Supper table, seeing my "enemies" seated next to me, all of us being loved equally by God. Another image that gave me courage and also freed me from mistakes and wounding behavior of the past was that of a beehive in my heart with golden bees making "honey of my old failures."[3]

Images have also reminded me how valuable a sense of humor is for healing. Mary Lou Sleevi portrays the widow Anna, in the Gospel of Luke, as the image of a woman who could laugh through the tough things of life: "Anna comes to Her Moment laughing. Those eyes have twinkled as she wrinkled. . . . Her face the free expression of all that's inside."[4] Perhaps, most of all, images have helped me to name my need to surrender and to trust God with my life. In order to be healed, I need a desire to let go, to get on with my life, rather than cling to the pain and memory of my old wounds. Some see surrender as negative because, for them, it implies a patriarchal approach to God, a giving in to a "higher power." I do not envision it this way. I see surrender as a natural part of the cycle of life and, thus, it includes the spiritual path as well. I have learned much about having to let go of control by observing seasonal surrendering such as the plowed fields of spring accepting heavy rainfalls, summer's fruitful days giving way to autumn harvesting, and winter's wind whirling snowflakes into banks of beauty. My surrender does not seem passive to me. Rather, it feels like a strong trust in a loving One whose wisdom stretches far beyond mine. God can empower me, work through me, and weave patterns that I do not dream possible. I experience this as a great gift of love.

A story from the Christian scriptures also led me into a profound surrender to God. When I thought that the grief over my father's death would never leave me, I found little comfort from being with the earth. I would walk and sit and look and gaze but I could only "be there." One day I decided to begin praying with the healing stories in the Gospel of Mark. On the day that I proceeded to pray the story of Peter's mother-in-law, I put myself into the story and saw myself as the woman lying on the bed. I visualized Jesus coming to her, taking her by the hand, and lifting her back up into life. As I saw myself being lifted up by Jesus, I had this instant flash of recognition: I was trying to heal myself by myself (that old independence of the head wound!) and my wound could be healed only by waiting, by surrendering, by believing that I would be lifted into joy again. I waited for six more months before this joy came back to me.

As I've experienced the wounds of midlife, the season of autumn has always comforted me. It has given me the courage I needed to continue to say goodbye to whatever kept me from growing:

> October sheds a few more leaves,
> autumn shakes the last oaks free;
> all around me the earth rustles,
> dryness and death are in the wind.
>
> my soul clings to the earthen sounds
> and nestles in October's arms;
> a lingering and a longing take over
> and I cannot get myself to go away.
> I want to stay forever in the woods
> because my grief has found a home.

the inner wounds are welcomed
and tears come and go freely.
all that hurts and pains in me
is befriended by October's smile.

surrender becomes more than a should,
quietly it forms a truth that sings,
telling my entire being how blessed,
this letting go and giving over.

I know the season of autumn is ending
as winter wraps the world in frost,
but deep inside I have found a friend,
and I know this bond will keep me warm. (P. J.)

Midlife: Woundedness and Healing

Several years ago a friend and I facilitated a weekend gathering on midlife. We decided to ask the group to focus on the two questions asked in the film *City Slickers:* "What was the best day of your life and what was the worst day of your life?" We weren't sure if the participants would be willing to share their "worst day" and, if they did so, what they might choose to share. We presumed that they would be reluctant to share their "worst day" because of the vulnerability of speaking about one's own woundedness, so we gave them an option to talk about one or both questions.

To our great surprise, every one of the forty participants focused on their "worst day" rather than on their "best day." Many of them spoke about experiences that had happened to them in their childhood or early adult years. I'll never forget all the pain of old wounds that I heard within the group. This tearful time of sharing was a tremendous moment of healing as each one described a time when they were deeply wounded. This experience opened my eyes to the fact that most adults carry unhealed wounds of some sort. Midlife is certainly a time when these wounds become more apparent and demand more attention.

Healing involves gathering together what has been lost, forgotten, repressed, disowned, and inviting it into one's life again. The Hebrew word that describes this welcoming what has been lost is *tikkun,* which means to heal or to mend what has been broken, to transform it.[5] When we tend our wounds in midlife, we invite the forgotten or lost parts of ourselves back into our life and let go of what does not belong to us.

Not all midlife persons are attentive to their old wounds. Some may hide from the wounds by surrounding themselves with hectic busyness, constantly shoving aside any reminders of what needs to be healed. Others may lack self-esteem and think either that they shouldn't hurt, or that their hurt is insignificant alongside someone else's hurt, or that they caused the hurt and therefore deserve to be pained. Some persons long to tend to their woundedness but cannot find the psychological or physical space to do so because of many family or work responsibilities. Some avoid their inner pain because they fear that loved ones will be hurt if they tend to such things as childhood abuse or other wounds connected to their family of origin. Others have deeply repressed the wounds and do not know the hurt is there until some other powerful issue forces them to look inside and see the wound.

Sometimes midlife persons do not face old wounds because they are fearful of stirring up too many old memories that might reinforce the hurt. Others fear discovering things about themselves that they don't like, or of doing difficult things like talking to or forgiving someone who's hurt them. There are also some midlife persons who have a "be strong" persona and try to manage their woundedness from an unemotional distance. Sooner or later, however, the wounds of the first half of life scream so loudly that this voice overpowers any of the rational or irrational reasons one has for avoiding the healing process.

Many authors recognize that there are certain aspects of healing that need to be a part of midlife growth: acknowledging the wounds and accompanying emotions, recognizing their source, being compassionate toward ourselves, letting go and being less in control, forgiving self and others, facing our fears, developing a sense of humor, surrendering to a divine presence greater than ourselves, and being patient with how slowly healing often happens while also being attentive to and caring for our body, mind, and spirit.

Imagery has always been an integral part of healing in the history of health, and it definitely influences how a person views his or her health and illness.[6] The same holds true for midlife healing of wounds of the spirit. Jean Houston trusts the use of imagery as a means of healing and uses song and story to invite and encourage this process. She believes that one's wounding is an invitation to renewal and that woundings "tell us that old forms are ready to die." It is in the wounding within one's own story that "the seeds of healing and transformation" may lie.[7]

Many midlife respondents used images to express dimensions of healing as a part of their journey and to describe how their healing had taken place. Here is one response:

> Water also healed me . . . many warm baths . . . lying on a mat in the pool in the hot sun and imagining the baptismal waters that brought me to new life were literally doing it again . . . in the shower, my prayer: "purify me, O God" as I feel the water cleansing both my body and my spirit. (Q.R.)

Another respondent indicated that her healing was like that of the jewels in a jewel box: "There are still a few unpolished rocks there and they are now in a rock polisher. . . . The jewels in the jewel box tell me that the hurts in my past life have really been turned into moments of grace for me" (Q.R.).

Music has also been a source of healing. The author William Styron, in his moving account of his deep depression, narrates how the image of a song in a film brought him out of a suicidal depression. He had begun to make necessary preparations for his death, like going to see his lawyer about his will, trying to write a farewell letter, etc. On the evening he planned his demise, he sat down to watch an old film that held a song that stirred his heart. This song led him to wake up his wife and tell her of his plan for suicide. Styron was hospitalized and recovered. He describes how the song stirred him:

This sound, which like all music — indeed, like all pleasure — I had been numbly unresponsive to for months, pierced my heart like a dagger, and in a flood of swift recollection I thought of all the joys the house had known: children... festivals...love and work...slumber...voices...All this I realized was more than I could ever abandon....I realized I could not commit this desecration on myself.[8]

Control issues in midlife were central to almost all of the respondents. Both men and women struggled with having to quit forcing things to happen, with giving up their independent self-efforts and allowing God to heal in them. A male respondent indicated that his career had not been fulfilling and added:

I am torn between how to make myself more a successful worker through man's definitions (work harder, work smarter, make a greater effort to get along with boss, etc.) or to accept my strengths and weaknesses...ask God to help me let go of my definitions of work, success and fulfillment. (Q.R.)

Issues of control accompany the call to let go of security, of things of the past, of whatever keeps one from future growth. As one woman noted: "Midlife is...the undoing of the life of the ego....as I surrender control, to that extent I am free and happy" (Q.R.). The authors of *Chaos or Creation* stress that all of this is out of our hands and that "we do not, cannot control the presence [of God] or this losing of control."[9] An image of a comforting God can be helpful in encouraging this healing process. A woman respondent described God as someone "who holds my hand and cries *with* me (rather than for me) when bad things happen" (Q.R.).

Another midlife respondent described how a failed pregnancy taught her that there were things beyond her control. It was "a shock" for her to learn that she couldn't completely control her life. Out of this experience, she said she no longer tries to create her own destiny. Lack of control was also expressed by another's image of "...being carried along by the waves, the tide pulling me in the direction I need to go. I have little real control; God is carrying me and it feels good" (Q.R.).

A similar image of letting go of control was that of a river: "How like the course of my life, which I too often entertain the illusion of controlling, only to discover that in surrendering to the flow I am carried safely by a greater power to my destiny" (Q.R.). Another respondent mentioned: "a sailboat, dependent on God's wind. Not out of control, yet not really in control because of dependence on the wind. I feel less need for control than earlier" (Q.R.). This attitude is also in the following comment:

> The greatest changes in my spirituality have occurred not by what I have done but in what I have un-done. . . . I have given over more and more of the idea that I really control anything. Control is another of the aggravating illusions of our time. (Q.R.)

Several midlife respondents mentioned safety issues in their struggle with trying to control their world. One woman wrote: "My old self needed to be in control to feel safe. I believed I was in control and could make everything happen in my life if I just tried hard enough. I was usually exhausted" (Q.R.). Similarly, "a safety net" came out of a man's fear of risk-taking and unemployment. He wrote: "At the time, I thought that I would be swallowed up by the earth if this or that happened to me. Well, obviously I survived, and am in better health than ever. Whenever old fears come to me, I visualize the safety net beneath my universe" (Q.R.).

As we proceed with our midlife healing, we may periodically have to pause and wait for the next step. A retreatant told me how she was walking in the Big Horn Mountain area when it was very muddy. She would gradually get laden down with mud on her hiking boots and could barely walk with their heaviness. She would have to stop and clean them off, shake the mud loose. She said this is how it is for her at times. She has to stop in order to clean off the accumulation, to shed that which has made her journey a lot slower because the accumulation on her "boots" gets so heavy.

Not all midlife persons readily admit to their fears and misgivings. It is natural to try to cut ourselves off from our feelings. We can try to hold the emotions in but this obviously does not work because the pressure is too great and the wounds, with all their pain, eventually rise to the surface. Acknowledging our feelings is a must if we are going to be healed.

Midlife healing usually insists that we return to the past, particularly to our childhood, spending some time there making peace with the past and putting some closure on it. Understanding our childhood is essential as we seek the truth about ourselves.[10]

Learning to love and appreciate ourselves is also an essential component of midlife healing. Self-esteem and self-love have often been considered either sinful or selfish by many. Instead, a positive self-image is vital for growth and healing.[11] This self-love and self-acceptance requires that one let go of certain expectations, either those of self or of others, and that we accept the goodness that is ours simply by our "be-ing" who we are.

The wounds of midlife persons may be large or small. Whatever size they are, some healing will need to take place. As it does so, the opening of one's spirit will begin to happen. We may not know this opening for a long time because it often develops slowly and imperceptibly, but one day we will look back on our midlife journey and see that the wounds we once wore are now only scars to remind us of that long process that once was ours.

It is through the process of healing that we become more accepting of ourselves and less fearful of who we are. When we bid farewell to our wounds, we regain the inner energy that has been focused on the hurt. It is often through facing our struggles and painful ordeals that we discover greater clarity and learn what gives our life direction and meaning. We perceive more fully what is truly of value and come to appreciate life at a new depth. And all the while, the enduring green moss continues to sing in our soul, urging us to come home to our true Self, the place of deep peace and love.

Simmering Time

1. With what images of healing do you most identify? Do you have images of your own that speak to your experience of wounds and healing in midlife?

~

2. Visit a wound of your past that you consider to be healed. How has this wound been your teacher? What wisdom did you receive from this woundedness?

~

3. Find a nature object, something of the earth, such as a leaf, a stone, a shell, a flower, a feather.... Sit with this gift of the earth. Stop your "head talk." Just *be* with the object. Touch it, hold it reverently. Listen to it. Hold it to your heart. Let it be a source of healing for you.

After you have spent at least twenty quiet minutes with this gift of the earth, take a pencil and paper, or paints, and draw what comes to you about your woundedness.

~

4. *Questions for journaling and/or discussion:*

   - What was the best day of your life? What was the worst day of your life?

   - In your midlife journey, what wounds have you discovered that have needed healing?

   - Who or what has been your "green moss," your source of courage and resiliency, during your wounded times?

   - How would you describe the process of your midlife healing?

~

5. Befriend the most significant wounds of your life:

   a. Call them to come to you.
      Gather them around you.
      (You might want to make a list of them.)

   b. Listen to what each wound says to you.
      (Their voices are heard best in your "gut.")

   c. Dialogue with any of them that seem especially raw and rough: ask each one these two questions: What have you done with me? Is there something I can do to help you heal?

After this exercise, draw a mandala of your experience of woundedness and healing.

~

6. Choose one of your wounds. Then ask yourself: If someone were sitting in a chair across from me and had experienced this woundedness, what approach to healing would I take with him or her?

~

7. Does the poem of Jessica Powers speak to your experience of woundedness and midlife healing?

> All that day long I spent the hours with suffering.
> I woke to find her sitting by my bed.
> She stalked my footsteps while time slowed to timeless,
> tortured my sight, came close in what was said.
>
> She asked no more than that, beneath unwelcome,
> I might be mindful of her grant of grace.
> I still can smile, amused, when I remember
> how I surprised her when I kissed her face.
>
> —JESSICA POWERS[12]

Has suffering ever stalked your footsteps? Have you ever kissed suffering's face? If so, how did this happen?

~

A Prayer for Healing

Healing God,
come to my hidden corners,
open the doors to my soul rooms
that are tightly locked.

Awaken in me.
Bring to life all my deadness.
Enthuse the depressed emotions.
Reenergize my inner weariness.
Bathe the grime of my ego-centeredness.
Clarify my confusions.
Fire my neglected loves.
Brush off my dusty dreams.
Nurture my spiritual hungers.
Ease my sore relationships.
Deepen my sense of self-esteem.
Stir up my connection with the world.

Tenderly gather in your arms
all that still needs healing,
all that remains wounded and wanting.
May I grow each day into greater wholeness
with a stronger, purer inner freedom.

—Joyce Rupp

CHAPTER EIGHT

Midlife Hope:
Discovering the Secret Garden

*It is only when we can believe that we are creating the soul
that life has any meaning, but when we can believe it — and
I do and always have — then there is nothing we do that is
without meaning and nothing that we suffer that does not
hold the seed of creation in it.*

—MAY SARTON

when midlife comes along
it is time to awaken
the dreams in us
that have nearly died.

it is time
to call them forth,
to remember
how it felt
to risk all
for the inner vision.

and the vision
has wings of wisdom now,
no more excuses
for why dreams
can't be tried.

it is time.

now or never.

dreams
if not lived soon
will die.
dreams
if not tried on
now
will fall apart
like beautiful clothes
left too long
in a rotting attic.

blessed be the One
who keeps on believing
in us

and blessed be the One
who goes on dreaming
in us
even when we forget.

—Joyce Rupp

I REMEMBER THE DAY that I saw the *The Secret Garden*. I knew the film's story well. Adventure-filled children discover a hidden, walled garden thick with trees and overgrown with wild vegetation. There, in that secret place of beauty, they bring a wonder-lost boy back to a healthy life. I loved this story and wasn't expecting any surprises when I went to see it. However, as I watched the children weed and clean the neglected garden and excitedly plant flower seeds in it, I felt a quiet stirring in my soul.

When the magic moment of spring returns to the gloomy English moor, the garden comes alive. The seeds the children have planted send out long stems of life from the soil. They shoot upward in slow motion, filling the screen with green. Buds form and, suddenly, before the viewer's eyes, magnificent flowers unfold into colorful glory. As the green in the garden leapt into life, tears streamed from my eyes. I couldn't stop crying. They were not tears of sadness. Rather, they sprang from some place deep inside of me that acknowledged my midlife journey and was full of gratitude for having survived the seasons of struggle. I felt as though I was the flowers in the garden that had been coaxed into life.

Like the children discovering a much-neglected place of beauty, in midlife I had found a garden within me that had needed attention and was now beginning to bloom. Like the children, I had found the key to this place and had given much inner work to weeding and planting. When the flowers in the film began to bloom, I felt those flowers come to life inside of me. They gave me a huge sense of hope and promise, confirming the value of my midlife journey as a source of personal transformation.

When I saw *The Secret Garden*, I had completely forgotten an image that had come to me eight years earlier. I uncovered it as I reviewed my journals:

In my spiritual journey, I have come time and again to a very tall wooden gate. I always knew there was this wonderful garden beyond it. I could smell the flowers as I stood before the gate but it was never open for me to enter the garden. Today as I read more in *The Cloud of Unknowing,* my prayer and my yearning seemed to be revealed. It is like the gate to the garden is slowly opening for me and I can walk in and see, ah, the beauty of the garden and the beauty within me. (P.J.)

Hope is not just one single quality or promise. Hope has to do with believing beyond today — knowing there's a garden of beauty that awaits me. Hope encourages me to follow my dreams, to believe in the part of me that envisions my wholeness. Hope is trusting that what is happening will eventually make sense, or if it never does become meaningful, it will still offer an opportunity for growth. Hope assures me each morning that my life is of value no matter how unsettling or disturbing my current situation is. Hope encourages my heart not to give up and nudges me when it's time to move on. Hope doesn't need words or proofs or conditions. Hope accepts mystery and offers the gift of solid trust in the unknown. Hope doesn't pretend that I'll get all I want nor does hope deny that there will still be struggles down the road. Hope tucks promises of growth and truth inside the pockets of my struggles.

As I look back at my midlife journey, I realize I would never be who I am and where I am today if it had not been for hope. In the midst of my many inner struggles, I had hope:

... of greater inner freedom when I felt strangled by my fears and weaknesses.

... of finding the truth of myself when I groped around in the cave of my darkness.

... of accepting my mortality when I encountered my own aging.

. . . of living my unspoken dreams even when I experienced failure and self-doubt.

. . . of living a more balanced life in the midst of my crazy busyness.

. . . of being at home with God as I shook off old ways of naming and relating to God.

. . . of being faithful to my significant relationships while I searched for the meaning of commitment and fidelity.

. . . of sharing my personal talents and gifts in a loving, generative way as I allowed myself to see my ego-centricity.

Today I see that each of these dimensions of hope has become a reality in my life. Not that it's all accomplished and finished. Far from it. But I know that each of my hopes is greening and growing. I have never completely lost hope, even in my darkest cave times. Always I have been able to reach inside and find a reason to continue the journey. Sometimes this hope has been fragile and hard to reach, but it has always been there. Many times I've found hope through things of the earth, or through something someone said to me, or through some passage that leapt at me from a page in a book. Sometimes it was just a whisper in my soul that promised me strength to get through the wilderness of my sadness and confusion.

In my thirty-eighth year I began a new journal and searched, as I always do, for a cover that would speak to what was predominant in my inner process. One day I found a close-up photo of a junco with its striking black hood, gray breast, strong beak, and deep black eyes. The bird was perched on a tiny twig and stood out all the more because the background of pink and yellow flowers was blurred in focusing on the junco. Emily Dickinson's poem leaped into my mind:

> Hope is the thing with feathers
> that perches in the soul,

And sings the tune without the words
And never stops at all...[1]

The junco and the poem connected to a space inside of me that both doubted and believed in myself and in my dreams. It was the space in me that was still in the dark soil but was slowly pushing a new green shoot up out of the ground. Little moments of hope, like finding the junco photo, happened over and over in my midlife journey. They sustained me and gave me energy to continue. These were the times when I felt at home with myself, believed in and trusted who I was. I welcomed those handfuls of hope like a desert traveler welcoming water.

Sometimes my finding of the secret garden of hope was just a momentary thing — my midlife search and struggle was far from over. Yet, I also knew that even quickly passing hope was a gift given to me so that I would have the strength to continue. Toward the end of my forties, I felt more and more hope and less and less struggle. I was more accepting of "the way life is" and felt much more at home with my own identity. I knew that it was time to let the past be, to turn it under like a farmer turns the spring soil over when a new crop is planted. I felt myself moving toward greater inner freedom and a oneness of body-mind-spirit. The season of springtime within me kept extending to longer and longer spans. It is no surprise that I closely identified with the external season of spring and found much hope in it. I would simply look at the signs of new life and feel a strong connection with my own inner growth.

A solitary row of tulips caused a stir in me. One long glance at them convinced me that I was also moving out of my wintertime. Hope is like that when it is real. An intimate touch of the deepest truth brushes through my memory and I know that I can never fully return to the shadows of yesterday.

Another year I found hope in an old, partly withered lilac bush. I first noticed her when the snow was still upon the land and wondered if she would ever bloom again. I decided that every morning I would visit her and "hold her hand" for awhile to encourage her growth as well as my own. I did this for three months until the lilacs were in bloom. Each of those days I felt a stronger confidence in my own return to life as well.

Learning "how life is," being willing to accept that life will always have its hills and valleys, allowing both light and darkness to live in creative tension within me, has also helped hope return to my heart. As I see this reflected in the earth, I find my own willingness to live with the tumbles and turns of life growing stronger.

Other images of hope in my personal journals have included:

- looking down at the pavement in amazement and seeing grass coming through the cracks, pondering how the urge to grow can push against concrete and find its way to the sun

- two rose bushes and their growth patterns, one blooming quickly and the other seemingly dead for weeks, waiting and waiting until finally a wine-colored shoot came forth

- a dream in which I was walking with a loving companion in a pastoral setting, seeing unicorns and being welcomed by a majestic figure

- working in a garden and seeing that the plants were blooming and bearing vegetables, even in hot, dry conditions when the ground was cracked and seemingly unable to produce anything

- going out in early morning to see a crocus and finding it had closed itself in the night, wrapped and protected itself against the cold; then, watching as the sunlight unfolded it

- standing under the stars on a summer's night, feeling at home, a tremendous connectedness with a world much vaster than my own, kneeling down and surrendering my life to God

- a maple seed resting in my hand, seeing the potential for growth, a future tree waiting to germinate

Another time that hope came slowly and steadily into my consciousness was in the wintertime in the midst of midlife pain and loss. Each morning that I walked out the front door to go for my crisp winter walk in the dawn, I heard a resounding chorus of sparrow chirps coming from inside a thick cedar tree. I couldn't see any birds, but I could hear all this "music" coming from the center of the tree. Every day that I walked past the tree, I smiled and wondered how the birds knew what time to wake up. I wondered if the internal alarm clock of my midlife journey would wake me up when it was time to move on. I came to look forward to these wee creatures' voices. Their sound sparked something inside of me and sang like an angelus of hope in my soul. It was several weeks later when I realized a heavy pall had lifted from my spirit. The "singing tree" had brought me a gift of encouragement.

Soaring swans in flight was also an image of hope. I stood amazed at their graceful unfettered flight; they moved forward as if their whole life was centered on a clearly seen goal. I felt that I had the power within me also to fly freely toward the future, with confidence, beauty, and integrity.

Scripture passages have also brought hope to my midlife heart. I had read the story of Noah and the flood many times but had not thought much about the symbolic dove that Noah sent out from the Ark to see if the rain had stopped. Then, one day, when I needed the gift of hope and a belief that the "flood" would end, I happened to be reading this story and saw, for the first time, what a powerful day it was for Noah when that bird came back with a sprig of green in its beak, telling them that there was a solid piece of land somewhere after all that time adrift at sea (Gn 8:6–12). I wrote in my journal:

> A small silent, pure white dove has arrived on the ledge of my life's window. A dove with a thin, green sprig of an olive branch — symbol of the new energy in me. A feeling of starting over, freshness. Yes, the season of hope has overcome me and in the grayness of early February, my heart turns toward greening things. (P. J.)

I have recognized the presence of hope in myself as I have grown less fearful of myself and others, as I've felt a greater openness to risk the unknown and the untried, as I've sensed more of a balance in be-ing and do-ing and given myself wholeheartedly in relationships. Images have helped me to do the patient waiting that is necessary in order for healing to come.

Another movement of hope within me has been the call to generativity. Daniel Levinson wrote that "the meaning of legacy deepens and the task of building a legacy acquires its greatest developmental significance" during midlife.[2] This has been my experience. I've become more aware of the legacy or contribution that I want to, and need to, leave for future generations. As the flowers of my inner secret garden have bloomed, I have experienced a growing awareness of my oneness with all of life and, consequently, of my responsibility to share of my person and giftedness with the world. The most significant aspect of generativity has been that of a call to compassion and generosity. Both the compassionate life and message of Jesus and the Buddhist practice of "lovingkindness" have become goals of mine.

This call to generativity has helped my life to take on purpose and meaning again. Many images related to generativity have helped me to gain both a clarity and an incentive toward compassion. I have seen myself bonded with all the creatures of the universe, looked closely at their uniqueness and their needs. I have felt drawn to images in the newspapers that tell of the pain and struggle of the people of the world. One day at the time of receiving the Eucharist at Mass, I had an experience that brought this truth very close:

> Just for the slightest moment today, only for a heartbeat of space, I was deeply united with those who have nothing. I walked to receive communion, held out my hands, open, ready to receive. Expectant. Nothing happened. No Bread. Empty plate. The priest turned away. That instant of emptiness will long linger with me. Complete dismay and loss until I realized that he was going back to the altar to bring more Bread back. And now I intensify that moment by tens of thousands. I see the starving ones with their hungry eyes and bloated bel-

lies. Skin stretched around piercing bones. Their hands need bread for body and they have none. My empty hands. I look at them now. They say to me, "You are so full always." How good, if only an instant, to have been left empty-handed, bread-less. (P. J.)

Other images of generativity and compassion have been an empty basket waiting for harvest, fire in my bones meant to be shared, the words of a song: "Love is the only power . . . give your love away," ripened fruit as a sign of my talents ready to be given in service, a house at night with light shining from all the windows calling me to be a presence and vision for others, an apple with the seeds in it reminding me of the potential for growth that I want to leave for others, my life as a holy shrine where men and women can come and feel a sense of peace and oneness, and my life as a womb where I can help generate life for those who need it.

This call to generativity has given me the incentive I need to accept the pain that comes with ongoing personal growth and the courage to be willing to "die a bit" in order to give of myself for the sake of those who will come after me:

> There are days
> when I dream myself
> to be
> dandelion to the last puff
> a full circling miracle
> hanging onto a fragile stem
> complex in my beauty
> yet simple in my standing —
> knowing I'll only grow again
> if each intricate
> delicate parachute of mine
> is pulled off, whirled away
> and seeded in
> some strange new soil. (P. J.)[3]

Midlife: Recovering Hope and Becoming Generative

What is it that keeps our hope alive and gets us through the tough things of midlife? I think that each of us has something or someone that gives us hope. This "reason for hoping" may be a person, or a special place, or a religious belief, or a vision of life that is strong enough to weather the internal storms and strife. There is an Ethiopian legend about a shepherd boy, Alemayu, that speaks to me of the power of hope. Alemayu had to spend the night on a bitterly cold mountain. He had only a very thin cloth to wear. To the amazement of all the villagers, he returned alive and well. When they asked him how he survived, he replied:

> The night was bitter. When all the sky was dark, I thought I would die. Then far, far off I saw a shepherd's fire on another mountain. I kept my eyes on the red glow in the distance, and I dreamed of being warm. And that is how I had the strength to survive.[4]

Each of us has a "shepherd's fire on another mountain" that has kept our hope alive. When the nights of our midlife have been dark and bitterly cold, we have seen something "far, far off" that has helped us survive. This "fire" has given us the courage to recover our lost self and to believe in the dreams that stir in our soul.

The time comes when we need to move on, when it is no longer appropriate or healthy to stay lodged in the darkness or the pain of past wounding. Slowly we move forward with a new understanding of how we are to live the second half of our life. Hope encourages us toward new beginnings.

Sam Keen opens his book *Beginnings without End* with a beautiful story about hope that could be applied to many midlife journeys. Keen tells about a dream that changed his life. In the dream, a man walked into his room: "He was strong and beautiful, a seasoned man who had fought many battles in the dark jungles of the world." This man came over, sat on the edge of Keen's bed, and said to him: "I have learned one important thing in life — how to begin again."[5]

Beginning again, with the wisdom we have acquired from going deeper and discovering who we have become and who we now are — this is a big piece of the hope that midlife offers to us. Sarah, woman of faith of the Hebrew scriptures, knew about hope. After she said yes to uprooting, leaving behind her security, trekking into the vast unknown, she gives birth to Isaac, a name meaning "laughter" (Gn 21:1–7). Isaac was the new beginning for Sarah. Isaac is a symbol of our own new beginnings. What is there in our life that we least expect will unfold? What "child" has come forth out of our midlife womb of darkness? Our Isaacs are varied and many: mended or newly discovered relationships, old dreams dusted off and brought to life, creativity that we never believed in before, a view of ourselves that is both beautiful and bountiful, a spiritual path that energizes us, a work that never seemed possible. There may be many "children" as a result of our midlife seeding — our "Isaacs" have unlimited potential.

As we receive the new life of our midlife journey, there is a call to share with others what we have received from our midlife process. Joseph Campbell refers to this power or inner gift as "an elixir" that the hero is given after he has made the descent into the depths and returned to the world. It is this elixir that is meant to transform the world. Campbell envisions this "return and reintegration with society" as "indispensable to the continuous circulation of spiritual energy into the world."[6]

As the second half of life proceeds, the view clears and a stronger sense of purpose evolves. "This combination, the knowledge of limits and the conviction of a future life task," forms the essence of a meaningful recovery from the midlife experience of losing and finding oneself.[7] Our generativity comes with a price: discovery of both our vulnerabilities and our strengths. It is out of this discovery that our generativity flows. Getting in contact with our own uniqueness and truth empowers us "to be true to Self and a leaven for others."[8] It is the discovery that one can be "tamed" without giving up one's strength, that one can be converted and unleash this strength "for healing the world."[9]

Midlife women who have finally come to love and appreciate themselves and are making healthy choices for their own personal growth may question generativity because "doing their own inner work" and choosing to follow a path that allows their gifts to be more fully used may feel selfish or self-oriented. It is good to remember that generativity begins with the discovery and the claiming of our own true selves. Many women have been giving constantly of themselves in a generative mode for most of their lives. These women have to recover their lost self first before they can continue to serve as catalysts for the world's transformation. Most women have focused their life on loving and giving. The time will come again, after the development of personal transformation, when women who have been faithful to their own inner process will once more turn their hearts toward generativity.

In *The Silent Passage,* Gail Sheehy believes women's experience and wisdom will be a significant gift to the future. She refers to the phenomenon of postmenopausal zest, a term coined by Margaret Mead and experienced by many postmidlife women. Sheehy sees the middle-aged woman moving into the position of healer in her later years of life.

One female respondent described generativity this way:

> As a teacher I recall the days of programmed learning, when each student worked at his or her own pace toward the goal of the unit. That is how I see my life. I have been given one set of learning activities. Each person has been given a different one.... There is no competition between us because our goal is the same.... The school we are all attending is the school of love. (Q.R.)

The "school of love" is the foundation of generativity for both women and men. According to Erik Erikson, generativity focuses on protecting, nourishing, and cherishing the next generation, including one's children, students, and protégés. The intention of generativity arises from two particular areas: an increased awareness of one's own mortality and a heightened sense of how one is united or bonded with all that exists.[10]

A male respondent explained that he used to have an image of himself as a father and a provider earlier in life but that this image had changed to now include "notions of teacher, leader, example for my children's spiritual journey" (Q.R.). Another man noted that he now has the central image of himself as "being a grandpa," being a mentor and witness for his grandchildren (Q.R.).

Hope and generativity imply a connectedness with a world that is much larger than us. Sue Monk Kidd compares generativity to Thomas Kelley's "cosmic mothers tenderly caring for all" or as being universal brothers and sisters, by which we "relate to the world in such a way that we see others not as strangers but as part of us," thus helping us to walk with them in their deep and wounded places.[11]

The experience of interconnectedness changes our perception of the world. Our relationship with the world becomes that of an extended self.[12] A woman respondent sensed this inner compassionate direction in her life: "I find that each year the delicate buds of spring mean more and I long to find more time just to savor the gifts of life. At the same time, I have a deep sense of anguish about much that is wrong in our world and I grieve over what could be, should be, and is not" (Q.R.).

Iris G. Fodor and Violet Franks pose the question:

> We need to ask whether midlife and beyond is to be feared as a loss of youth and opportunity, a time for closing down and drying up; or is it a new prime of life, a time of renewal, getting rid of youthful preoccupations with appearance and body, a time to seek out new challenges, valuing wisdom, maturity, and new possibilities for growth and change.[13]

There are other aspects of generativity. One is that we become less frantic and work-oriented and more at ease with just "being." This gift is seen as "a time of ripening... — mellowing and deepening. Like a piece of fruit on the tree — the energy before midlife seems to have gone into the growing — becoming more full and complete . . . less activity involved in becoming and much more concern with 'being'" (Q.R.). Yet another aspect of hope and generativity is that of acting in a more ethical manner. As one respondent put it: "striving to be able to speak and act from my core in a spiritual and ethical sense" (Q.R.).

Relationships tend to become of vital importance as midlife moves into hope. Many respondents expressed how much more important relationships are to them now than in the past. Some move from being very independent or dependent to being more interdependent. Others are just beginning to realize how much certain people mean to them. I found this in a woman who values other women as mentors, the man who wants to be a good grandpa, a woman who finds church community very encouraging and supportive, another who visits her aging parents more often and enjoys friends more, and a number of women who speak about finding "spiritual sisters."

Joseph Campbell also reflects on the value of relationships and offers hope for the journey when he reminds us that we do not have to risk the adventure alone, that heroes (and heroines) of all time have gone before us. He states that the labyrinth is known and we have only "to follow the thread of the hero path." Campbell notes that we shall eventually "come to the center of our own existence" and "where we had thought to be alone, we shall be with all the world."[14]

Perhaps the biggest piece of hope is that, in midlife, we have the opportunity to come home to ourselves. Parts of us that were lost are found and now give us new vitality for the future. Laurens van der Post tells a beautiful story of the little bushman, Hans Taaibosch, in *A Mantis Carol*. This little bushman came to live in the United States. While he basically adapted to this life, he always had a great hunger to return to his homeland. This hunger is a tremendous longing that is buried deep in the hearts of all the bush people when they are away from their place of origin.

Van der Post poignantly describes the bush people returning to the land that they have cherished and have always longed for in their hearts:

These old people pressing their wrinkled cheeks against the rocks, fondling the boulders, stroking and touching all round them tenderly with the tips of their fingers and weeping bitterly as if they were long lost things found after a heart-breaking search.[15]

This intense longing to go home was the "great wound" of Hans Taaibosch and it often filled him with loneliness. The great hunger was the deep desire in him to return to where he most truly belonged. Sometimes this little bushman would dance the "Dance of the Great Hunger," a dance of longing for one's homeland. He knew that he could only return to the land in spirit and so the most effective way was to dance out his longing, to look on the place of his origin with love, "to dance this deep, deep pattern of departure and return."[16]

In midlife we awaken to our own longings for a homeland that is deep within us. Hope helps us to gather the courage to travel there and to search for the part of us that we unknowingly have longed for all our lives. This is the place where our dreams dance, where our passion for life gestates, and where the person we are meant to be cries out for recognition. While this longing within us for our true Self is never fully satisfied in this life, midlife urges us to accept the longing and to discover what we can. As we come to know more of our true Self, we too touch these hidden parts of ourselves as tenderly as the bush people did. We too dance the "Great Hunger Dance" as we journey in hope of finding ever more of our true Self, as we keep calling "Dear Heart, Come Home!"

Simmering Time

1. What image of hope most relates to your own midlife experience of hope? Do you have other images that speak of hope to you?

~

2. Have you discovered an "Isaac" in your life? If you have, how has this "Isaac" affected your life? What happened in order for you to birth this new dimension of yourself?

~

3. Have you experienced a "shepherd's fire on another mountain"? What keeps you going in the hard times? Make a list of your reasons for hoping. Write these on a kite or on a windsock or a helium balloon. Fly them freely.

~

4. Write a dialogue with one of your hopes or dreams for your life or draw your secret garden.

~

5. What would a dance of hope look like? What would a song of hope sound like? Create one of these. Listen to music that brings hope to your soul. Participate in some form of art and beauty.

~

6. *Questions for journaling and/or discussion:*

- If someone were to say to you: "Speak to me of hope," how would you respond?

- What keeps you from having hope?

- What happens when you feel your hope is dashed? How have you recovered your hope?

- Describe a time in your life when you felt hope return to you.

- What are the hopes that encourage your life now?

~

7. When Vera Stravinsky was ninety-one years old, she was asked her secret. She answered: "It's all very simple. I work, I travel, I never let anybody scare me, and I take great pleasure in the beautiful things in life."[17]

What is your "secret" or vision of life? What motivates you to live your life in the way that you do?

You might write a dialogue with Vera Stravinsky. Ask her more questions about her midlife journey. Let her help you with the "secret" of life.

~

A Hope-Full Prayer

Stream of Love
all encompassing
gathering me
as a cherished one
in welcoming embrace

Stream of Compassion
bonding with me
holding my tears
in the tender cup
of your love

Stream of Goodness
pouring your light
into my soul
like a sunbeam
at dawn

Stream of Nurturance
providing for me
in the darkness
of your protective
enveloping womb

Stream of Joyfulness
dancing in me
celebrating life
with each moment
of gladness

Stream of Mercy
receiving my sorrow
with understanding
as you continue
to believe in me

Stream of Hope
ever glorious
ever present
kissing my vision
and enriching my dreams

—JOYCE RUPP

CHAPTER NINE

Conclusions

*Tell me. What is it you plan to do with your one wild and
precious life?*

—MARY OLIVER

W HEN I FIRST BEGAN HIKING in the Rocky Mountains, I
was on a trail I'd not traveled before. It led to a spectac-
ular lake surrounded by cliffs. It was not a particularly
difficult path, but I was not used to the altitude and my midlife
body was doing a lot of huffing and puffing. I had stopped to rest
at a place where I needed to climb over some boulders in order to
continue upward. I had no idea of how much farther I had to walk,
but I was getting weary and worn out.

Just then, a family came bounding down the path. In the lead
was a small girl about six years old, long blond hair swinging in
the breeze. She was as alive and alert as I was winded and half-
dead. She stopped when she reached me, looked at me with great
compassion and exclaimed, "It's not much further. It's really worth
it. You're almost there!"

I will never forget those words. They echoed in my spirit the
rest of that day and far beyond. They reminded me of how much
I need others to help keep my dreams alive. I also heard those
words as the voice of my divine companion, encouraging me and
promising me that the midlife journey to my true Self would be
well worth the effort. It truly has been.

As I have reflected on the midlife journey to the deeper places
within myself, I see how so much peace has come to me because of
what I have learned. Each of the following discoveries has, in one
way or another, been a part of my process. I found many of these
to be present also in the respondents' Midlife Questionnaires and
in their comments at the Midlife Gatherings. I believe that these

elements of growth are possible for any person who is willing to go deeper.

As we journey inward during midlife, we may discover:

- that our persona probably has chinks and cracks in it and may need some mending or adapting, or a complete renovation.

- that we can find wisdom in the wounds we've carried from birth onward, and that these wounds can heal.

- that surprises of beauty and talent in us wait to be discovered and shared with the universe.

- that some of what we thought to be unbreakable truth, beliefs, and values is now shattered pottery and unmendable.

- that risk-taking is essential if we are to grow.

- that we are loveable as we are.

- that loneliness need not kill us.

- that we require time and solitude for ourselves.

- that dreams not lived now never will be.

- that we must come to terms with the reality of our mortality and stop pretending that our bodies will never die.

- that the best of who we are has not only survived the bruises and battering of life's storms but has actually taken root and is ready to put out a vivid green shoot of life.

- that many of our efforts to hide in the clutter of busy activity have left a dry, stale taste in our soul and we are crying out to be held in the embrace of simple presence.

- that we have within us the weaknesses we've despised in others.

- that what we saw as our failure was really our teacher.

- that guilt and shame can be kept for only so long before they turn sour.

- that past regrets must be let go lest they cling to us and suck our energy for life like leeches in a farm creek.

- that the loving part of us can always out-wrestle the hating part of us.

- that our struggle to name God and to find a spirituality that enlivens and enriches our existence is less complex than what we first thought.

- that we can be free as a child to enjoy the wonder of life in a simple, spontaneous splashing of play in the world.

Some Words of Encouragement for Those in Midlife

A large percentage of the respondents felt enthused and encouraged about their lives. I believe this is due to the fact that many of them were at a point of completing their midlife process and could look back to see how they had grown.[1] Enthusiasm and gratitude usually come *after* one has spent some time in the confusing, stretching, dark times of the transformation process.

One of the respondents shared her encouraging words for other midlife persons by telling of a dream she had:

> As I fussed about how long therapy was taking, I was given a dream. I was lying in a courtyard, naked, when I realized the watchman was closing the gates. I scrambled to gather my clothes, dash to a shelter to dress and slip out, before he would notice me or close the last gate. But in my panic I fell headlong to the ground and when I looked up he was standing over me. With the most loving look and in the gentlest of voices he said, "Take all the time you need to get dressed and, whenever you are ready, I will let you out of the gate." (Q.R.)

As I conclude my reflections on my own midlife journey, I find myself feeling grateful because I, too, have been given the time I needed to go out of the midlife gate to freedom. I have experienced the deep embrace of a divine presence and feel confident that every part of my spiritual path has been for my teaching and my growth. I also understand that I will be stretched and challenged in the future. At the same time, I feel confident that I will be comforted

and loved into an ever greater clarity of who I am. There is no
need to be worried and anxious about gathering my spiritual gifts
and hurrying my growth. I need only to tend my "one wild and
precious life" and the rest will be given, in time, in time.

> when the time is ripe,
> the vision will come.
> when the heart is ready,
> the fruit will appear.
> when the soul is mature,
> the harvest will happen.
>
> not to worry
> about all the unspoken,
> the unnamed, the undelivered.
> not to hurry
> the sprouts out of seeds,
> the weeds out of garden.
>
> let it all grow.
> wait for the ripening.
>
> yearn for the yielding
> if you must,
> but be patient,
> trust the process.
>
> talk to the restlessness,
> sit with confusion,
> dance with the paradoxes,
> and sip tea
> with the angel of midlife.
>
> smile while you wait,
> empty basket in hand,
> all too eager
> to snatch the produce
> of your spiritual path.

—JOYCE RUPP

Appendix A

Midlife Questionnaire

1. How would you describe what "spirituality" is *for you?* (Your own understanding of spirituality rather than how "the experts" would describe it.)

2. What chronological years would you define as your "midlife years" (e.g., 35–40, 40–55,...)? _____ Describe your experience of midlife.

3. Have you noticed any changes in your spirituality during your midlife years? If yes, please describe those changes.

4. How do you feel about your spirituality in your midlife years?

5. Have any significant images been a part of your midlife journey? If yes, please list some key ones and describe how these images have affected or influenced your midlife process.

6. What image *most describes* your spirituality during your midlife years? (You may have already described this image in detail with question #5 and will just need to note here which one it is. Please tell what makes this particular image so significant for your midlife journey if you have not already done so in question 5.) Anything else you want to add about this image and its significance for your midlife journey?

7. What advice or suggestions would you give to those in midlife regarding their spirituality?

Midlife Themes from My Journals

As I reviewed my journals I found major midlife themes weaving in and out of the pages, year after year. These themes included the following:

1. *Struggle:* countless inner battles, stress, tension, anxiety, desert and wilderness images.

2. *Search:* feeling lost, having no maps or direction for spirituality, fear of the unknown.

3. *Loneliness:* issues related to sexuality, spiritual longings for God, restlessness, sense of not belonging.

4. *Darkness:* periods of depression, confusion, inner "dyings."

5. *Disillusionment:* disappointments, change of beliefs and values, lost dreams, evaluation of life, family of origin and religious traditions.

6. *Mortality:* personal aging, death of loved ones, illness.

7. *Clarity:* insights, revealed truths, greater meaning, new sense of direction.

8. *Grief:* death and relationship breaks, emotions associated with grief such as sadness, anger, self-pity, depression.

9. *Be-ing/Do-ing issues:* success orientation, sense of failure, the push to be productive, longings for deeper contemplation.

10. *Generativity:* stronger sense of connection with all of life, development of compassion, desire to use personal abilities in a lasting way.

11. *Letting go:* continual recognition of the need to yield or surrender, control issues, the call to trust God.

12. *Hope:* encouragement and energy related to the earth and the seasons, seeing personal growth, positive sense of the future.

13. *Limitations:* recognition of the Shadow, Ego/Persona issues, physical aging, evaluation of goals and dreams, struggle with personal weaknesses.

14. *Interiority:* intense search for truth and clarity, stronger focus on the inner world, dreams.

15. *Healing:* longing for wholeness, naming of old wounds, recovery of instinctual nature, trusting intuition, willingness to move on.

16. *God-relationship:* desire for union, struggle to "name" God, questions of how to pray, emptiness and dryness, the move toward contemplative prayer, constant relationship to Nature, acceptance of Mystery.

17. *Relationships:* friendships, commitment decisions, balancing extroversion/introversion.

Question 7: A Summary of Responses

Question 7 of the Midlife Questionnaire was as follows:

"What advice or suggestions would you give to those in midlife regarding their spirituality?"

The responses had many similarities and thus are grouped into thematic or topical areas.

1. Seek and search. Be true to self. (More respondents commented on this than on any other topic.)

- Make sure the path you are on is right for you. Respect all paths. Listen to your heart. Be true to yourself. Explore your unique path in order to find meaning. Find out who you are and why you are here.

- Don't be afraid to explore and question your spirituality. Address your negative feelings and experiences that you have about religion and spirituality. Work with them.

- Keep questioning. Make certain you are open to new ways of thinking. Reexamine, learn, research, change. Be open and aware. Take risks. Be aware of choices. Learn to choose, without apology.

- Realize that you are doing the best you can and that's enough.

- Give yourself something to be really passionate about.

- Ambiguity is our friend. Hang loose. Let it be.

2. Prayer, meditation, solitude, or time apart.

- Let your mind and heart rest apart from busyness each day. Spend more time being quiet. Listen to the inner voice.

- Cut back on your activity. Set aside an extended time to get in touch with your midlife journey. Practice some sort of daily prayer. Visit your spirituality in a more focused way at intervals.

- Go within. Keep returning to the center, to what is basic for you. Allow God to strip you of everything else.

- Don't be discouraged if it seems spiritually you're moving one step forward and two steps back. Remember you are still praying even when it doesn't seem like it.

- Before you do anything else, let God love you.

- Don't try to control meditation. Keep trying to "let go and let God." Don't be afraid to lose control.

3. Individual or group support.

- Be a part of a spiritual growth group. Find a church community where you can give freely and fully.

- Connect and reach out. Don't do it alone. We were not made to make this journey alone. Find a companion, someone who's trustworthy and reliable. Go with a companion into the dark. Find a wise spiritual director.

- Don't be afraid to reach out for help and understanding. Let others know how you feel. Share your life experiences so others can learn from them.

- Cherish your friends.

- Honor your elders. Find and treasure older mentors who will help to awaken you.

4. Face struggles and fears.

- Don't be afraid of crisis when it manifests itself. Struggle with life. Don't give up.

- Believe that God is here even when you don't sense this. Find comfort from knowing God is asking you to become more spiritual. Keep going. Look to God for direction.

- Be patient. Realize that "this too will pass." Take as long as you need. Don't give up because you go through a time where the quest is on the back burner. Trust the process, as painful and agonizing as it might seem to be at times.

- Don't be deterred by thinking that suggests that if you have not laid the groundwork during your earlier years you cannot reap the benefits in midlife. Maybe only those of us who have failed hopelessly can be receptive to a new way of thinking about spirituality.

- Forgive yourself for past sins, failures, and disappointments. Accept imperfections; recognize the good that is there.

- Give up the task of trying to judge how "successful" you are. Let go of others' expectations. Befriend your Shadow.

- Live with your fears and go ahead anyway.

- Learn to lean into your pain, loneliness, grief, confusion, hurt, even despair.

- Honor the feminine. Learn to balance the masculine and feminine in yourself.

5. Kindness to self.

- Be gentle with your life. Don't be hard on yourself. Let it happen in its own time. Do not try to force it or try to deny it. Give yourself time and space. Go easy on yourself.

- Be good to your body. Stay healthy. Exercise. Treat your body with TLC. Baby yourself — you deserve it. Listen to your body's needs; exercise regularly.

- Slow down. Learn to play. Don't always try to analyze life. Enjoy life and hold it in deep reverence.

- Live with humor. Laugh a lot! Laugh, laugh, laugh. One good "guffaw" before 10:00 a.m. each day. Don't take yourself too seriously.

- Always relate to children in some way. They know the secrets of the journey already. Watch for the thousand little serendipities that God sends, every day, to surprise and bless us.

- Trust the process. Trust yourself. Trust God.

APPENDIX D

Rituals for Midlife Gatherings

(These opening and closing rituals can be used when a group is gathering to discuss the chapters in the book. For each ritual, a candle is lit and placed in the center of the group unless otherwise indicated. A chant is suggested for each gathering. It is helpful to chant for at least three minutes. All chants are found in Appendix H [p. 179]. At the conclusion of each opening ritual, bow to God who dwells in one another.)

Chapter 1

Opening:

a. Have some roots, or photos of roots, in the center of the group or ask the participants to bring a photo of someone who helped to give them roots. Place these photos in the center of the group.

b. Invite the group to join in the chant "O, I Open to You" (p. 179).

c. Stand in a circle of solidarity, holding hands. Invite and honor the ancestors by asking the group to call out names of those they have known either personally or through history — i.e., the "roots" who have given wisdom and guidance to them.

Closing:

a. Begin with a brief time of silence. Then invite the participants to speak a word or a phrase from the group's sharing that is most comforting and helpful for the journey of going deeper.

b. Read the quote from Teilhard de Chardin that is at the close of the chapter (p. 33).

c. Pray the prayer at the end of the chapter.

An alternative for the closing of each gathering is to lead the group in the Guided Visualization suggested for the chapter (Appendix I, p. 182).

Chapter 2

Opening:

a. Have an unlit candle for each participant in the middle of the group.

b. Chant "Come a Little Further" (p. 180).

c. Invite the group to sit quietly and reflect on their times of darkness. Then ask each to come forward, one at a time, and light a candle as a sign of hope when in darkness. Repeat the chant once after each candle has been lit.

Closing:

a. Sing "Song of the Dragon" to one another — one group being the dragon and the other the child (p. 178).

b. Pray the closing prayer at the end of the chapter.

Chapter 3

Opening:

a. Have a variety of maps around the lit candle.

b. Chant "Looking Down the Road" (p. 179).

c. Have small cards in a basket on which are labeled words of hope (e.g., vision, laughter, enthusiasm, strength, integrity, spontaneity...). Invite each one to come forward, choose a card, and take some time to ponder the word. Each one then calls out the word they have received.

Closing:

a. Stand and walk slowly in a circle while chanting "Looking Down the Road" as a sign of walking into new inner territory.

b. Pray the prayer at the end of the chapter.

Chapter 4

Opening:

a. Arrange a variety of green plants around a lit candle.

b. Read the following psalm verses:

> Let me abide in your tent forever, find refuge under the shelter of your wings. (Ps 61:4)

> O God, in you my soul takes refuge, until the destroying storms pass by. (Ps 57:1)

c. Stand in a circle, arms on the shoulders of the person on either side. Chant "Shelter Me" (p. 179).

Closing:

a. Sit and chant "Shelter Me."

b. Invite the participants to name persons who have stood by them in their times of loss, grief, and darkness.

c. Pray the prayer at the end of the chapter.

Chapter 5

Opening:

Have many baskets of all sizes and an unlit candle in the center of the group.

a. Chant "Darkness, Silence" (p. 180).

b. Each participant is invited to take a basket, hold it, look into the emptiness and remember times of spiritual emptiness. The leader then prays: "We hold these baskets, confident that our desire to receive your energizing life and love is enough to offer you, God. In our empty times, help us to trust that the days of filling and harvest will come again."

c. The candle is then lit. Each one comes forward to place his or her basket around the candle. As each one does so, he or she proclaims: "I believe my empty times can be my teacher."

Closing:

a. Chant "Darkness, Silence."

b. Call out names of God.

c. Pray the closing prayer at the end of the chapter.

Chapter 6

Opening:

a. Place skins (or photos) such as a snake-skin, crab shell, chrysalis, tree bark that's peeled off, discarded shells of seeds, fallen leaves, etc. around the lit candle.

b. Chant "Let Go, Come In" (p. 180).

c. Invite each in the group to silently write his or her name on an index card, to look at their own name, ponder who they, and who others think they are; reflect on what needs to be let go, what needs to be welcomed...

d. Place the names around the candle with the skins.

e. Chant "Let Go, Come In" for a few times.

Closing:

a. Create a skin-shedding dance. Invite the group to join you.

b. Pray the prayer at the end of the chapter.

Chapter 7

Opening:

 a. Place a variety of "healing remedies" such as bandages, ointments, etc. around the lit candle.

 b. Chant "Singing Our Soul Back Home" (p. 181).

 c. Think of a healing word or phrase. Go around to each one and whisper this word or phrase in the other one's ear.

Closing:

 a. Chant "Singing Our Soul Back Home."

 b. Invite participants to recall something in their life that has been healed. Then invite them to pray in gratitude such as "Thank you for . . ." or "I give thanks for . . ."

 c. Pray the prayer at the end of the chapter.

Chapter 8

Opening:

 a. Place a vase of fresh flowers and some packets of seeds in the center, along with the lit candle.

 b. Chant "I Am On My Way" (p. 181).

 c. View the scene of the garden coming alive in the film *The Secret Garden* (available on video).

 d. Each one then receives a flower to hold. Pause for a quiet time to receive and celebrate hope.

Closing

Have a card available for each participant. On one side of the card print the Mary Oliver quote on p. 157 above. On the other side, print one of the one-line responses in the summary to Question 7 (see Appendix B, p. 162 above) Place the cards in the center of the group, with the Mary Oliver quote facing up. Each participant chooses a card and then reads the one-line response. After each person reads the one line, the total group responds by naming the participant and saying: "_____, enjoy your one wild and precious life!" Conclude with group and individual hugs.

A Midlife Ritual Based on the Myth of Inanna

Begin by lighting a candle in the center and then inviting the participants to come and light smaller candles placed around the large one (one candle for each person).

1. *Inanna is Queen of the Upperworld, or Queen of Heaven:* Briefly review Inanna's life. Note Inanna's wealth and power, which is comparable to our ego and external successes, who and what has given us power. Then the participants are invited to write their name on a card (or to look at their name on their name tag or driver's license) and to ponder their own name: "Who am I and what power do I have?" After a pause, each one comes forward and places her or his name on a table or altar as symbols of "who we think we are." (ego/persona)

2. *Inanna chooses to descend to the underworld:* Inanna tells her helpers to come after her if she is not back in three days. Pause to reflect: "What has taken us, driven us, invited us to go deeper into darkness, to go where we've not been before?" Take quiet time to ponder this inner movement.

3. *Inanna goes through the seven gates:* She loses all her treasured possessions that gave her power. She goes into the darkness naked and alone. Pause to reflect: What has been asked of us in "letting go"? Then sing the first part of the chant "Let Go, Come In":"Let go, let go, let go some more, let go of everything, God is All" (p. 180).

4. *Inanna dies in the underworld:* Ereskigal, Queen of the Underworld, wails and mourns. "Name some of the emotions as you have experienced the grief and loss of midlife." (Participants call these out to the group.) During this time all the candles are blown out and all lights in the room are turned off.

5. *Helpers come and bring Inanna back to life:* Let us ponder our helpers, our guides, our mentors, those who have "brought us back to life."

6. *Inanna is revived and returns* but must spend one-half time of every year in darkness or send someone in her place. "What are some of the wisdoms you have learned from your darkness?" Each participant shares a wisdom and then comes forward to relight a candle. Following this, sing the second half of the chant "Let Go, Come In": "Come in, come in, come in some more, come in, I welcome you, God is all" (p. 180).

7. *Conclusion:* The leader speaks: "We have gone with Inanna to the underworld and have come back from the descent. Let us now turn and offer a blessing of hope to those around us as we conclude this celebration of our inner transformation."

A Celebration for a Woman's Fiftieth Birthday

Each of the invited guests is asked to bring:

a. a candle

b. a story of an older woman (either living or deceased, either personally known or from history, literature, etc.) who has been a mentor for her.

Gather in a circle as the leader shares information and descriptions of the Crone archetype — the third dimension of the Triple Goddess (maiden, mother, crone), the symbol of the Aged Wise Woman.

Do some circle dances and/or sing some songs to the Great Mother. Gather again in a seated circle around a table that has one large candle in the center. The leader begins by acknowledging the Light that each one present brings to the celebration and lights the center candle to honor this common Gift of all present.

Following this, each one present is invited to share her story of an older woman who has been a mentor. After the story has been shared, she goes to the table, carrying the candle that she has brought with her. As she lights this candle from the center candle, she says: "I light this candle to honor..." and names the woman of whom she has just spoken, leaving the candle on the table to join the other light there.

The stories and the placing/lighting of the candles on the table continue until all have been shared. The leader then invites the group to sit in silence for a time to ponder and to remember all that has been shared. After a time of quiet, comments and responses are welcomed from the group.

The group again stands and sings a song and/or dances a circle dance. Then the one who is celebrating her fiftieth birthday comes to the center of the circle and stands or sits by the table filled with Light. Each one in the circle speaks to the birthday person and offers her the blessing of whatever central gift it was that she has received from her Crone mentor, e.g., "Sara, I offer you the blessing of a sense of humor" or "Sara, I offer you the courage to live your dreams." (As each one speaks the blessing, she can come forward and touch the birthday person's head or heart or hand.)

Close with a birthday song and refreshments!

Song of the Dragon

Song of the Dragon

Joyce Rupp

Chants

O, I Open To You

Joyce Rupp

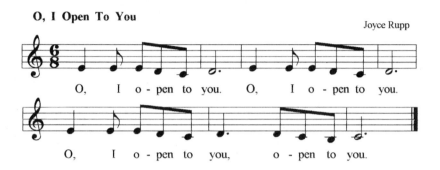

O, I o - pen to you. O, I o - pen to you.

O, I o - pen to you, o - pen to you.

Shelter Me Under Your Wings

Joyce Rupp

Ooh_____ Ooh_____

Shel - ter me un - der your wings. Shel - ter me un - der your wings.

Looking Down The Road

Joyce Rupp

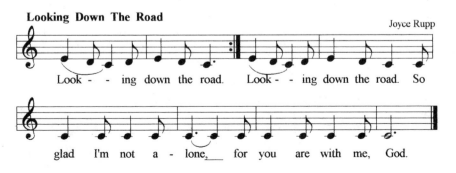

Look - - - ing down the road. Look - - - ing down the road. So

glad I'm not a - lone,___ for you are with me, God.

Darkness, Silence

Joyce Rupp

Dark - ness, si - lence, with no light to be seen.

Help me be - lieve you are with me, God.

Let Go, Come In

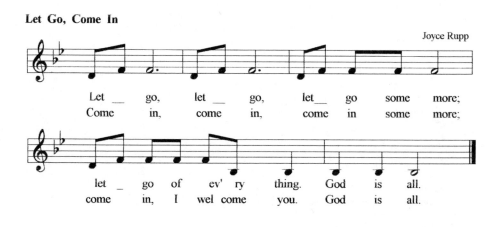

Joyce Rupp

Let ___ go, let ___ go, let ___ go some more;
Come in, come in, come in some more;

let ___ go of ev' ry thing. God is all.
come in, I wel come you. God is all.

Come A Little Further

Joyce Rupp

Come _____ come a lit - tle fur -ther;

Come _____ come a lit - tle deep - er.

I Am On My Way

Joyce Rupp

I am on my way._____ I am on my way._____ Pass-ing o - ver,_____ pass-ing o - ver,_____ pass - ing o - - - ver.

Singing Our Soul Back Home

Joyce Rupp

Oo_____ Sing - ing our soul back home.

Appendix I

Guided Visualizations

The following guided visualizations can be read to you by a friend or recorded on tape for your reflection. They can also be used for the closing of a Midlife Gathering and read by the leader.

Begin each time either by lying down or by sitting in a comfortable chair. Relax by (a) being attentive to your breathing, (b) imaging yourself being filled with peace and light, (c) feeling yourself enfolded in love, embraced by a loving presence. Then begin the journey inward...

Chapter 1 / "Roots"

Picture yourself in a forest with tall, old trees... they have long limbs, heavy brown bark, and huge gnarled trunks... sunlight glitters through their dark green leaves... go and sit at the foot of one of these trees... lean your back against the trunk... feel the bark against your skin... sense the presence of the tree, its energy and vitality, its aged wisdom... as you sit, you look around and notice that some of the roots of the tree are partly above the ground... they are thick, dense roots, with a heavy protective covering...

There is one root next to you. You reach out your hand and place it on the root... feel the strength of the root... sense its ability to carry water and nourishment to the tree... notice how grounded it is in the earth even though it is partially in view above the ground... as you continue to place your hand on the root, you feel the root move slightly... then you hear a gentle whisper. It is the voice of the tree root speaking to you. It greatly desires to tell you something of significance for your life.

Listen closely to the root. What does the root tell you about your midlife process?... What does it whisper about your interior journey? ... (*longer pause*) Ask the root any questions you'd like about your journey of life. Stay with the root for as long as you wish ... (*longer pause*) When the root has finished speaking with you, touch the root gently in gratitude ... bid the root farewell and visualize yourself leaning back against the tree again in silence and peacefulness ... stay by the tree and let the wisdom you have received sink into your soul. When you are ready, allow yourself to come slowly back to this time and place.

Chapter 2 / "The Cave"

See yourself going down a path ... you come to a very dark woods ... you see someone, a Wisdom figure ... this Wise One embraces you like a long lost child ... looks lovingly into your eyes ... asks to be your Guide ... takes your hand ... you go into the forest together ... deep, far, long ... you come to a cave in the forest where it's darker yet ... you can only know your way by holding onto the Wisdom person's hand ... you smell the cave ... feel the walls ... the floor ... listen for sounds in the cave....

You come to a large stone in the cave ... the wise Guide invites you to sit down there ... the wise Guide encourages you to talk about your difficult life situations. You tell this One about your darkness while the Wisdom person listens intently to you ... (*a longer pause here*).

You can see the light in this Wisdom person's eyes, shining in the dark as the eyes look upon you warmly ... then the Wisdom person gives you a treasure box ... it is not very large and feels very light ... you feel it ... hold it ... you can't really see it ... but you can feel the lid ... you open the box slowly ... it is filled with radiant, loving light ... the light comes slowly out of the box and surrounds you, fills you, permeates you and the wise Guide, like stardust sprinkled all through you ... receive this light ... enjoy it ...

The Wise One takes your hand ... although you can both see easily in the dark now, together you walk out ... you say farewell ... you leave, carrying the box knowing the light is with you ... now gradually come back to this time and place.

Chapter 3 / "The Guide"

Visualize yourself in a wilderness...it is mid-afternoon and the scorching sun is beating hot rays on the land...you see large stones, dry, dusty sand, the lack of green...smell the dryness... feel the rough sand and the stones beneath your feet as you walk along...you look around and see that ahead of you is open space with few trees and little vegetation...feel the wind as it picks up speed and blows strongly across the sand....

You turn around and look at where you have been walking. You see that your footprints are already erased by the wind...you realize that the path you have been on is no longer there and the way back is not visible to you. There is no clear path ahead. You know that you are lost...you find a large rock to sit by, to protect yourself from the hot sun and wild wind...you try not to panic although you are sweating, hungry, and thirsty...you wait for some sign of another person to appear...no one comes...

Evening slowly descends and you find yourself in darkness... you feel the cold now that the sun is no longer shining...you hear the sounds of creatures in the wilderness...let yourself sit in this night space...you finally fall asleep and rest in this wilderness. See yourself asleep by the rock...you awake to feel the first glow of rising sun on your face...as you yawn and stretch, you see a white-robed person sitting near you...you sense an immense peace coming from this person...

The white-robed Guide is looking at you with fondness and with deep compassion....The Guide reaches into a pack and brings out water and food for you. Then the Guide speaks to you: "I have been with you through this night although you could not see me. I am here to guide you on your way. Will you let me be with you? I know the way through this wilderness. I know how to help you take care of yourself as you travel here. Will you trust me?" Take some time now to respond to the white-robed Guide...(*a long pause here*).

Now the white-robed person looks upon you with deep, loving affection...offers a hand to you...you take it and the two of you rise together... then you both slowly move ahead into the wilderness... as you do so, you sense that you will be protected, cared for, and nourished by this Guide... deep down you know that you will be safe on this journey... gradually let yourself return to this time and place.

Chapter 4 / "Remembering and Letting Go"

Go to a forest... it's green and alive with birdsongs... walk into the forest... go to a waterfall... at the bottom of the waterfall is a large stream of water... there's a spring of warm, delicious water there. Nearby is a sweet scented apple tree in bloom... either lie down by the edge of the stream and place your arm in the water... or if you are comfortable with this posture, lie down in this water up to your shoulders... you can feel how soothing and comforting the warm water is...

An angel of God is with you. The angel lies down next to you, side by side, so close that the two of you touch one another... the angel is there to give you comfort, strength, support... you can feel the warmth and kindness of the angel... the angel promises to be with you... you lie there with the angel close to you...

You remember a childhood wound, a time when you were hurt or disappointed or abused verbally or physically, when some negative message got into your head that influenced you into your adult life... feel the comfort of the angel... the beating of the angel's heart... with the help of the angel, send this message down the stream... see it flow along, out of the stream, into an ocean... there it is dissolved in the great waters...

You remember a hope of yours that has gone away, a dream of yours that you long to hold in your heart but seems to be far away from you now... recall what might have chased this hope away (a fear, busyness, doubting your own goodness, others' opinions of you... feel the love of the angel, which is like starlight... feel the vibration of goodness from the angel's presence... now send whatever keeps you from living your hope and your dreams into the creek waters... see it flow along, out of the stream, into an ocean...see this hindrance being dissolved there in the great waters...

You remember someone you loved who has died or a relationship that has come apart and cannot be mended...take note of your feelings about this experience...sense the deep compassion of the angel's tears dropping silently upon your cheek...gather any lingering sadness, bitterness, anger, hurt...send this into the stream...float it down into the ocean...

You remember how your body looked and felt at age twenty-five...you see how it has aged...gather any negative feelings you may have about this...feel the angel's smile of happiness looking at your mature body...sense the total acceptance of the angel's love for you...take any negative feelings you may have about your body and float them down the stream...out into the ocean...see them being dissolved...

You remember anything else that is caught in your heart and keeps you from peace and joy...feel the compassionate love of the angel's presence next to yours...sense the glow of care in the angel's breathing...gather these things that keep you from being your truest, most peaceful self and send them into the stream...see them float away, into the great waters of the ocean...

You lie there on the green grass and suddenly you hear the quiet movement of feet upon the grass near you...the spirits of those in the forest gather around you...they hum a gentle melody for you...cradling your spirit with their love...you know deep within you: all shall be well, all shall be well...let yourself be in their gentle embrace for awhile...then they slowly move away and you hear the soft whisper of their feet in the distance, gone now...the angel blesses you, leaves you with what you need for the second half of your life...you arise from the stream, touch the water for one last time, receiving the blessing it has to give you...you leave the water and slowly return to this time and place.

Chapter 5 / "Beloved of God"

See yourself as a very young child (one–three months old)...you are in a wooden cradle. It is a very sturdy cradle, finely made, with delicate carvings on it...there is a hand-knit blanket over you and a small pillow under your head...notice the wonder of your tiny body (hands, feet, eyes, soft skin...)...notice how fresh and alive you are...the cradle is hung on a strong branch of a pine tree...you can smell the tree's fresh scent...a gentle wind blows...you can hear it in the trees...feel the cradle move slowly with the rhythm of the wind...feel yourself rocked back and forth, back and forth, back and forth by a gentle wind...soft muted sunlight comes through the tree branches and falls on your face...feel the tender warmth...let it sooth your cheeks...bathe your forehead in kindly light...

You are untainted...untouched by worry, care, concern...you are content just to "be"...to be rocked by the gentle wind, back and forth, back and forth, back and forth...your mind is clear... you receive each moment just as it is...your heart is completely open...it is filled with love for all of life...let yourself be rocked ever so gently, comfortingly...stay with this...now you sense that the wings of God are wrapping your cradle with love...you are being bathed with a tender love...it is the love of God...let this love embrace you...let this love rock you back and forth, back and forth...

Lovingly and gratefully see your adult self lift this child from the cradle...and place the child in your heart...let the child's freshness, love, clear mind, and pure heart permeate your inner being...welcome this child into the depths of yourself...bring this child back with you now, to this time and place...slowly, gently...return to this time and this place.

Chapter 6 / "Skin-Shedding"

It is midnight. There is a full moon...you are in a green, verdant meadow in late springtime...the air is warm, just right for a walk under the moonlight...you slowly meander through the meadow...it is easy to see your way because the moon is bright... you pause and smell the wildflowers — a sweet fresh odor...you smell the night air...you see a grassy clearing in the meadow and you walk over to it...you find a spot to lie down on...the grass is soft and downy, very comfortable...your body feels safe and protected here...smell the greenness of the grass...you gaze at the moon...feel the energy...

As you lie there, you think of the part of your life that no longer works for you, whatever it is that gets in your way and keeps you from growing...(*longer pause here*) See this part of you as a skin tightly wrapped around you...what does this skin look like?...what does it feel like?...this is the part of you that binds you...keeps you from moving...from going where you want to go...now envision yourself growing too big for this old skin...it's getting dry and transparent...it's slowly separating from the rest of you...feel yourself sliding around, trying to shed the skin...see how you brush against the grass, push against the earth...slowly you slip out of the skin that no longer fits for you...what does this feel like?...See the skin lying there beside you...it's empty, hollow, useless...

Continue to lie there now in the moonlight...feel the freshness, the freedom, the cleanness...let the vulnerable, exposed you be bathed in the loving moonlight...and now, from the soft light of the moon comes a divine being...the divine presence comes to you and kneels beside you...this presence leans over and breathes on you...receive the breath of new life...let it permeate you...the divine being lifts you to a sitting position...the two of you sit together...what does the divine being say to you about your skin-shedding?...(*longer pause*) Stay with the presence until you are ready to return to this time and place. When you are ready to return, receive a blessing from this divine being, and then gently leave the meadow and come back to this room.

Chapter 7 / "The Healer"

You are sitting under a huge oak tree . . . the limbs stretch way out across the hillside . . . the tree has green, thick leaves, heavy branches, sturdy bark . . . the sun is shining with gentle warmth . . . there is a light breeze . . . birds are chirping and warbling in the tree . . . what does it feel like to be there? Be with this feeling . . . you stretch out on the grass beneath the tree . . . you are on your back facing up to the tree . . . just lie there in peace and quiet for a bit . . .

As you lie there you begin to think about your inner pain . . . call one of your wounds or hurts of your heart to you . . . give this wound a name . . . listen to this wound's pain — what does it say to you? . . . (*longer pause*) If you can, gather some of the love that enfolds you and place it around this wound . . . offer compassion and kindness to your wound . . . continue to lie there with your wound . . . as you do so, you hear footsteps . . . now, kneeling beside you is a great Healer . . . (this might be Jesus, or Buddha, or Mary, or your Guardian Angel, or someone else) . . . sense the power of healing in this person . . .

The Healer very intently and carefully assesses your wound . . . now the Healer tenderly and carefully takes the wound from you and holds the wound in a loving embrace . . . what happens to the wound? . . . the Healer looks again at you . . . the Healer touches you with Power . . . allow this healing power to move through you . . . receive it and welcome it into your whole person, body/mind/spirit . . . the Healer invites you to sit up . . . then the Healer lifts you to your feet . . . the two of you begin to dance under the great oak tree . . . and now the Healer embraces you . . . bids you farewell . . . you say goodbye . . . come back to this time and place.

Chapter 8 / "The Gift of Hope"

See yourself someplace in the past . . . another era of time . . . it might be as a Native American or early settler or in another culture of a much earlier era . . . you are with a group of loving people . . . they are a happy, compassionate, free group . . . notice how each one looks...what they are doing...what they say...one of the people who is a wise leader invites you to the center of the group...the people form a circle around you...hear them chant a blessing upon you...

The people invite you to a large pool of water...they ask you to slip into the water and be cleansed...take your time to go into the water, feel the fresh washing of your whole being...(*longer pause*). Come back out of the water...the people walk close around you in a loving, guardian way...they take you to a very large tree...it is tall and has a great hollow space at the bottom...it is large enough for you to sit down in and to feel enclosed by the tree...you go into the tree...hear the murmur of the heart of the tree...smell the tree's wood and the earthiness...sense how the tree responds to you...you close your eyes and rest with the tree...(*longer pause*).

When you open your eyes, there is a gift of HOPE before you ...what is the gift?...receive the gift...embrace the HOPE it holds for you...now you prepare to leave the tree...gather the gift of HOPE to your heart...thank the tree for the gift of HOPE given...the group comes and surrounds you once more...you feel their love...their eyes gleam with happiness for you...together you walk back to the place where you first met them...you bid each one farewell...slowly return to this time and place.

Notes

Preface

1. Susan Shaughnessy, *Walking on Alligators* (San Francisco: HarperSan-Francisco, 1993), 17.

Introduction

1. Janice Brewi and Anne Brennan, *Celebrate Mid-Life* (New York: Crossroad, 1988), 99.

2. Jack Kornfield urges "no boundaries to the sacred" when he writes of the spiritual path: "To fulfil our spiritual life we must cease dividing our life into compartments.... Spiritual practice can easily continue the pattern of fragmentation in our lives if we set up divisions defining what is sacred and what is not" (*A Path with Heart* [New York: Bantam Books, 1993], 184–85).

3. Irene Claremont de Castillejo, *Knowing Woman* (New York: Harper and Row, 1973), 87.

4. Sherry Ruth Anderson and Patricia Hopkins, *Discovering the Feminine Face of God* (New York: Bantam Books, 1991).

5. All excerpts from my personal journals printed in this book will be indicated by "P.J." (Personal Journal).

6. Mircea Eliade, *Images and Symbols* (Princeton, N.J.: Princeton University Press, 1961), 20.

7. Ibid., 11.

8. Kathleen Fischer, *The Inner Rainbow* (New York/Ramsey, N.J.: Paulist Press, 1983), 7.

9. Forty-eight women and twelve men responded. They ranged in age from thirty-six to sixty-six and were from a variety of religious traditions including United Methodist, Presbyterian, Sufi, Roman Catholic, Episcopalian, Native American, and Buddhist. Some had no religious affiliation. Of these respondents, fifty-two participated in the small group gatherings. Almost all of the respondents were professional persons who were generally well-educated. They were risk-takers — a woman in her mid-forties was in medical school, pursuing a dream she had greatly desired. In the first group I met with, every woman had had a major career change in the past ten years.

10. The questionnaire as it was given to the respondents is in Appendix A (p. 161). Both the questionnaire and the Midlife Gatherings were extremely helpful to me. Many of the responses from the questionnaires are included in the second half of each of the chapters of this book.

Chapter 1 / Midlife Interiority: Going Deeper

1. It is Thomas Merton who writes that when we find God we find our true self and when we find our true self we find God. This statement of Merton's, probably more than any other of his wisdoms, has had a tremendous influence on my life (see Thomas Merton, *New Seeds of Contemplation* [New York: New Directions Publishing, 1961]).

2. Many in midlife have had similar experiences in a different way. The call may not have been in a physical desert but in something like the desert of divorce, or job loss, depression, the last child leaving home, or entrance into a drug addiction recovery program.

3. Throughout the chapters, "Q.R." (Questionnaire Response) is used to designate all material from the Midlife Questionnaires.

4. Sue Monk Kidd, *When the Heart Waits* (San Francisco: Harper and Row, 1990), 8.

5. Nor Hall, *The Moon and the Virgin* (New York: Harper & Row, 1980).

6. William Bridges, *Transitions* (Reading, Mass.: Addison-Wesley, 1980), 45.

7. Janice Brewi and Anne Brennan write: "It is to the 'within' and 'the more than' that mid-life...beckons. The stirrings...move us to turn our attention to the voice from that inner world that has been speaking our self from the first moment of conception.... No matter how little or how much of our personality has been developed, there is still a whole other side of us left undeveloped.... It is a call to wholeness, the call to go beyond what we know of ourselves and to gradually encounter all the myriad aspects of ourselves, to discover the depths of who we are, and to integrate the polarities and contradictions that are found within us and contribute to our vitality and uniqueness" (*Celebrate Mid-Life* [New York: Crossroad, 1988], 32–33, 83).

8. Teilhard de Chardin, *The Divine Milieu* (New York: Harper and Row, 1957), 76–77.

9. Ibid., 77.

10. Merton, *New Seeds of Contemplation*, 38.

Chapter 2 / Midlife Darkness: Entering the Cave

1. I have written about this in more detail in *Little Pieces of Light* (Mahwah, N.J.: Paulist Press, 1994).

2. Dragons are mythical creatures. They have been used by Christians to portray an evil or negative force that must be slain or overcome. In many legends there is a cave with a pool of water where a treasure is hidden. The treasure is guarded by a serpent or a dragon. The dragon must be slain in order to obtain the treasure (Robert Frager and James Fadiman, *Personality and Personal Growth* [New York: HarperCollins, 1984]).

In earlier history, dragons were viewed much more positively as wisdom creatures. In Asia, dragons were envisioned as friendly creatures who brought good things to people. To this day the Chinese believe that certain dragons have the power to prevent evil spirits from spoiling the new year and that they can control the rainfall that is needed for crops.

Anne McCaffrey, science fiction author of the series *The DragonRiders of Pern*, presents a view of dragons as highly sensitive and loving creatures. Likewise, dragons are held in esteem by shamans, who consider the dragon as one of the many "power animals" who serve as guides and energizers for the spiritual journey. More recently, Lenora Black has written of the dragon as a symbol of the Holy Spirit; see "The Holy Spirit, Dove or Dragon?" *Spirit and Life* (May/June 1994): 10–12.

3. For the complete song, refer to Appendix G.

4. May Sarton, *Journal of a Solitude* (New York: W. W. Norton & Co., 1973), 147.

5. Murray Stein, *In Midlife* (Dallas: Spring, 1983), 21.

6. Ibid., 3

7. Ibid., 8.

8. Ibid, 9

9. Ibid., 45

10. Joseph Campbell, *The Hero with a Thousand Faces* (Princeton, N.J.: Princeton University Press, 1949), 12, 30.

11. Jean Shinoda Bolen, *Goddesses in Every Woman* (New York: Harper and Row, 1984), 289.

12. Maureen Murdock, *The Heroine's Journey* (Boston and Shaftesbury: Shambhala, 1990), 1.

13. Marcia Starck and Gynne Stern, authors of *The Dark Goddess: Dancing with the Shadow* (Freedom, Calif.: Crossing Press, 1993), write of women being forced to make this type of descent when such things as physical illness, depression, or major life decisions push them to uncover suppressed emotions. Women choose this descent when they want to make

contact with the unknown, shadow side of themselves and make efforts to do this.

14. Nor Hall, *The Moon and the Virgin* (New York: Harper and Row, 1980), 8.

15. Marian Woodman, *The Pregnant Virgin* (Toronto: Inner City Books, 1985), 15.

16. Rabindranath Tagore, *Gitanjali,* no. 78 (New York: Macmillan & Co., 1913), 94.

Chapter 3 / Midlife Searching: Old Maps No Longer Work

1. Robert Morneau and Regina Siegfried, eds., *Selected Poetry of Jessica Powers* (Kansas City: Sheed & Ward, 1989), "Abraham," 66.

2. Chapter 5 focuses on my midlife experience of imaging God and the changes in my God relationship that developed for me during this period of my life.

3. Stephen Levine, *Healing into Life and Death* (New York: Doubleday, 1987), 39.

4. Nor Hall, *The Moon and the Virgin* (New York: Harper & Row, 1980), 147.

5. Janice Brewi and Anne Brennan, *Mid-Life Directions* (New York/ Mahwah, N.J.: Paulist Press, 1985), 10.

6. Sue Monk Kidd, *When the Heart Waits* (San Francisco: Harper & Row, 1990), 19, 29.

7. Ann Bedford Ulanov, *The Wizard's Gate* (Einsiedeln, Switzerland: Daimon Verlag, 1994), 28.

8. A mandala is a very old form of gathering what is stirring in our psyche or our soul. The word itself comes from Sanskrit. Begin by drawing a circle — this is the container for what is stirring within you. Sit with the empty circle in silence, or with quiet music. Let thoughts and feelings come to the surface. What image (color, form, shape) most speaks to you? Begin by placing this in the center of the circle. Continue to add other images, colors, etc. as you ponder your inner world. After you have completed your mandala, give it a title.

Chapter 4 / Midlife Grief: The Tolling of the Black Bell

1. May Sarton, *Journal of a Solitude* (New York: W. W. Norton & Co., 1973), 22.

2. The Crone is a mythic figure symbolizing wisdom and self-assurance. She can be challenging and is always intriguing. She symbolizes the third

stage of the Triple Goddess (maiden or virgin, mother, and crone). The Crone has sometimes been depicted as a dangerous and ugly witch because of her ability to tell the truth and to confront the falseness of life. My understanding of the Crone is the depiction of a generative, older woman with inner power who is not afraid to stand in her truth or to challenge others with it.

3. The details of this celebration of an "Entrance into the Crone-dom" are in Appendix F and could easily be adapted for anyone wishing to have a similar ceremony.

4. Raymond Studzinski, *Spiritual Direction and Midlife Development* (Chicago: Loyola University Press, 1985), 96.

5. Roger Gould writes that after the death of a parent "the world is a different place. For a period of time it is emptier, lonelier or less meaningful" (*Transformations* [New York: Simon & Schuster, 1978], 228).

6. Peter O'Connor, *Understanding the Mid-life Crisis* (Walpole, N.H.: Stillpoint, 1981), 67–68.

7. William Bridges, *Transitions* (Reading, Mass: Addison-Wesley, 1980), 52.

8. Gould, *Transformations*, 218.

9. May Sarton, *Journal of a Solitude* (New York: W. W. Norton & Co., 1973), 79–80.

10. Janice Brewi and Anne Brennan, *Celebrate Mid-Life* (New York: Crossroad, 1988), 30.

11. Steven A. Galipeau, *Transforming Body and Soul: Therapeutic Wisdom in the Gospel Stories* (New York/Mahwah, N.J.: Paulist Press, 1990), 135.

Chapter 5 / Midlife Prayer: When the Bush Doesn't Burn

1. See Exodus 3:1–7, where Moses experiences the presence of God in a burning bush.

2. Marcus Borg, *Meeting Jesus Again for the First Time* (San Francisco: HarperSanFrancisco, 1994).

3. *The Star in My Heart* (San Diego: LuraMedia, 1988) describes in great detail my meeting and my love of Sophia.

4. The Wisdom literature of the Hebrew scripture has numerous references to Sophia, the Greek name for Wisdom. These passages include: Proverbs 1:20–33; 4:5–9; 8:1–36; 9:1–6; Wisdom 6:12–17; 7:7–14; 7:22–30; 8:1–18; 9:9–11; 10:1–21; 11:1–26; Ecclesiasticus 1:9, 10, 14; 4:12–18; 6:18–31; 14:20–27.

5. Julian of Norwich, *The Revelations of Divine Love* (New York: Doubleday, 1977), 33.

6. Katherine Marie Dyckman, S.N.J.M., and L. Patrick Carroll, S.J., *Chaos or Creation* (New York/Mahwah, N.J.: Paulist Press, 1986), 134.

7. Elizabeth Johnson, *She Who Is* (New York: Crossroad, 1990), 65.

8. See Raymond Studzinski, "Images of God," in *Spiritual Direction and Midlife Development* (Chicago: Loyola Press, 1985), chap. 4, 103–10.

9. I personally felt blessed by the discovery of this myth. I found numerous feathers at a time when I was in a significant segment of midlife growth. I first found an unusual colored feather as I stepped out of my car. Several days later, I reached into the outside pocket of my purse and found a tiny black feather there. That night I attended a lecture and the woman in front of me had on feather earrings. "Enough!" I said. One week later I had my final discovery of feathers and a good laugh when I found a small brown feather in my bathtub!

10. Anne Brennan and Janice Brewi, *Mid-Life Directions* (New York/Mahwah, N.J.: Paulist Press, 1985), 67.

11. Sherry Ruth Anderson and Patricia Hopkins, *The Feminine Face of God* (New York: Bantam Books, 1991), 64.

12. Studzinski, Raymond. *Spiritual Direction and Midlife Spirituality*, 109.

13. Anderson and Hopkins, *The Feminine Face of God*, 145.

14. The Diaries of Etty Hillesum, *An Interrupted Life* (New York: Washington Square Press, 1985), 96, 214.

Chapter 6 / Midlife Transformation: Shedding the Skin

1. See *The Descent to the Goddess* by Sylvia Brinton Perera (Toronto: Inner City Books, 1981), and the works of Diane Wolkstein for more details of this story.

2. Kathleen Norris, *Dakota* (New York: Tichnor & Fields, 1993), 130.

3. Some persons mistakenly think of "Shadow" as our sinful side. I understand the Shadow to be anything in our psychological makeup that is unknown to us or that we refuse to accept about ourselves. Thus, the Shadow reveals not only our potential destructiveness and our negative or flawed aspects but also reveals the goodness of ourselves.

4. See Mark 8:26–39. The author describes this man as being possessed by demons, living in the tombs with no clothes on, secured by chains that he would always break and escape. Jesus meets this possessed person and heals him.

5. Emma Jung writes: "If the possibility of spiritual functioning is not taken up by the conscious mind, the psychic energy intended for it falls into the unconscious, and there activates the archetype of the animus. Possessed

of the energy that has flowed back into the unconscious, the animus figure becomes autonomous, so powerful, indeed, that it can overwhelm the conscious ego, and thus finally dominate the whole personality (Emma Jung, *Animus and Anima* [(Dallas: Spring, 1957], 14).

6. Ibid.

7. I also discovered my "positive animus," the inner masculine that helped me with perception, logic, insight, and discipline. These were vital helps that I had also inherited from my father, and I found them essential in my life as a writer.

8. May Sarton, *Journal of a Solitude* (New York: W. W. Norton, 1973), 150.

9. William Bridges, *Transitions* (Reading, Mass.: Addison-Wesley, 1980), 100.

10. Anne Brennan and Janice Brewi, *Mid-life Directions* (New York/ Mahwah, N.J.: Paulist Press, 1985), 19.

11. Kathleen Noble, *The Sound of a Silver Horn* (New York: Fawcett Columbine, 1994), 40.

12. Michael P. Nichols, *Turning Forty in the Eighties* (New York: W. W. Norton & Co., 1986), 27.

13. June Singer, *The Gnostic Book of Hours* (San Francisco: HarperSanFrancisco, 1992), 17.

Chapter 7 / Midlife Healing: What the Green Moss Told Me

1. Three years later I discovered a newly published book with commentaries by Gloria Feman Orenstein on the work of Betty LaDuke. Feman Orenstein notes the following about the African Healer: "This magical, mythic mother... reveals the powers of the moon, the sun, the stars, and the all-seeing eye.... This one image unites psychic healing, physical mending, male and female, and all animals and plants.... The rhythm rises and mounts upward from the earth as the energies are channeled through the healer's body.... These energies, whose prime source is the Earth, heal the healer as well as the person seeking healing" (*Multi-cultural Celebrations: The Paintings of Betty LaDuke 1972–1992* [San Francisco: Pomegranate Artbooks, 1993], 118).

2. Clarissa Pinkola Estes, *Women Who Run with the Wolves* (New York: Ballantine Books, 1992), 338.

3. From a poem of Antonio Machado as quoted in Linda Schierse Leonard, *Witness to the Fire* (Boston: Shambhala, 1990), 340.

4. Mary Lou Sleevi, *Sisters and Prophets* (Notre Dame, Ind.: Ave Maria Press, 1993), 54–56.

5. Patricia Hopkins and Sherri R. Anderson, *The Feminine Face of God* (New York: Bantam Books, 1991), 223.

6. Jeanne Achterberg, *Imagery in Healing* (Boston: Shambhala, 1985), 7.

7. Jean Houston, *The Search for the Beloved* (Los Angeles: Jeremy P. Tarcher, 1987), 105–6.

8. William Styron, *Darkness Visible* (New York: Random House, 1990), 64–65.

9. Katherine Marie Dyckman, S.N.J.M., and L. Patrick Carroll, S.J., *Chaos or Creation* (New York/Mahwah, N.J.: Paulist Press, 1986), 20.

10. Raymond Studzinski, *Spiritual Direction and Midlife Development* (Chicago: Loyola University Press, 1985), 97.

11. Bernie Siegel, *Love, Medicine and Miracles* (New York: Harper and Row, 1986), 66.

12. Jessica Powers, "Suffering," *Selected Poetry of Jessica Powers*, ed. Regina Siegfried and Robert Morneau (Kansas City, Mo.: Sheed and Ward, 1989), 106.

Chapter 8 / Midlife Hope: Discovering the Secret Garden

1. Emily Dickinson, *Selected Poems and Letters of Emily Dickinson* (Garden City, N.Y.: Doubleday Anchor, 1959), 79.

2. Daniel Levinson, *Seasons of a Man's Life* (New York: Alfred A. Knopf, 1978), 221.

3. Originally published in *Alive Now* (Upper Room Publications), March–April 1980.

4. Jane Kurtz, *Fire on the Mountain* (New York: Simon & Schuster, 1994).

5. Sam Keen, *Beginnings without End* (New York: Harper & Row, 1975), ix.

6. Joseph Campbell, *The Hero with a Thousand Faces* (Princeton, N.J.: Princeton University Press, 1949), 36.

7. Murray Stein, *In Midlife* (Dallas: Spring, 1983), 121.

8. Janice Brewi and Anne Brennan, *Celebrate Mid-life* (New York: Crossroad, 1988), 11.

9. Dwight Judy, *Healing the Male Soul* (New York: Crossroad, 1992), 23.

10. Allan B. Chinen, *Beyond the Hero* (New York: G. P. Putnam's Sons, 1993), 69.

11. Sue Monk Kidd, *When the Heart Waits* (San Francisco: HarperSan-Francisco, 1990), 201.

12. Joan Halifax, *The Fruitful Darkness* (San Francisco: HarperSan-Francisco, 1993), 138.

13. Violet Franks and Iris G. Fodor, "The New Prime of Life? — Women in Midlife and Beyond," *Psychology of Women Quarterly* 14 (1990): 445–49.

14. Campbell, *The Hero with a Thousand Faces*, 25.

15. Laurens van der Post, *A Mantis Carol* (Covelo, Calif.: Island Press, 1975), 116.

16. Ibid., 116

17. Stanley Kubelka, *Over Forty at Last* (New York: Macmillan, 1980), 29.

Chapter 9 / Conclusions

1. A summary of these responses to the questionnaire is found in Appendix B.

Bibliography

Achterberg, Jeanne. *Imagery in Healing: Shamanism and Modern Medicine.* Boston: Shambhala, 1985.

Ammitzboll, Marianne. "Menopause: A Natural Rite of Passage: Women's Voices at Midlife." M.A. diss., Institute of Transpersonal Psychology, Palo Alto, Calif., 1990.

Arrien, Angeles. *The Four-fold Way: Walking the Paths of the Warrior, Teacher, Healer and Visionary.* San Francisco: HarperCollins, 1993.

Barbach, Lonnie. *The Pause: Positive Approaches to Menopause.* New York: Dutton, 1993.

Black, Lenora. "The Holy Spirit, Dove or Dragon?," *Spirit and Life* (May–June 1994): 10–12.

Bly, Robert. *Iron John: A Book about Men.* Reading, Mass.: Addison-Wesley, 1990.

Bolen, Jean Shinoda. *Goddesses in Everywoman: A New Psychology of Women.* New York: Harper & Row, 1984.

Borg, Marcus J. *Meeting Jesus Again for the First Time.* San Francisco: HarperSanFrancisco, 1994.

Brewi, Janice, and Anne Brennan. *Mid-Life Directions: Praying and Playing — Sources of New Dynamism.* New York/Mahwah, N.J.: Paulist Press, 1985.

———. *Mid-Life: Psychological and Spiritual Perspectives.* New York: Crossroad, 1987.

———. *Celebrate Mid-life: Jungian Archetypes and Mid-life Spirituality.* New York: Crossroad, 1988.

Bridges, William. *Transitions: Making Sense of Life's Changes.* Reading, Mass.: Addison-Wesley, 1980.

Campbell, Joseph. *The Hero with a Thousand Faces.* Bollingen series XVII. Princeton, N.J.: Princeton University Press, 1949.

Chew, Peter. *The Inner World of the Middle-aged Man.* New York: Macmillan, 1976.

Chinen, Allen B. *Once upon a Midlife: Classic Stories and Mythic Tales to Illuminate the Middle Years.* Los Angeles: Jeremy P. Tarcher, 1992.

———. *Beyond the Hero: Classic Stories of Men in Search of Soul.* New York: G. P. Putnam's Sons, 1993.

Clift Dalby, Jean. *Core Images of the Self: A Symbolic Approach to Healing and Wholeness.* New York: Crossroad, 1992.

Clift Dalby, Jean, and Wallace B. Clift. *The Hero Journey in Dreams.* New York: Crossroad, 1988.

Courtenay, Bryce. *The Power of One.* New York: Ballantine Books, 1991.

Castillejo, Irene Claremont de. *Knowing Woman: A Feminine Psychology.* New York: Harper & Row, 1973.

Cramer, Kathryn D. *Roads Home: Seven Pathways to Midlife Wisdom.* New York: William Morrow & Co., 1995.

DeShong Meador, Betty. *Uncursing the Dark: Treasures from the Underworld.* Wilmette, Ill.: Chiron, 1992.

Dickinson, Emily. *Selected Poems and Letters of Emily Dickinson.* Garden City, N.Y.: Doubleday Anchor, 1959.

Dyckman, Katherine Marie, S.N.J.M., and L. Patrick Carroll, S.J. *Chaos or Creation: Spirituality in Mid-life.* New York/Mahwah, N.J.: Paulist Press, 1986.

Eliade Mircea. *Images and Symbols: Studies in Religious Symbolism.* London: Harvill, 1961; Princeton, N.J.: Princeton University Press, 1991.

Estes, Clarissa Pinkola. *Women Who Run with the Wolves: Myths and Stories of the Wild Woman Archetype.* New York: Ballantine Books, 1992.

Fischer, Kathleen R. *The Inner Rainbow: The Imagination in Christian Life.* New York/Ramsey, N.J.: Paulist Press, 1983.

Frager, Robert, and James Fadiman. *Personality and Personal Growth.* New York: HarperCollins, 1984.

Franks, Violet, and Iris G. Fodor. "The New Prime of Life? Women in Midlife and Beyond." *Psychology of Women Quarterly* 14 (1990): 445–49.

Galipeau, Steven A. *Transforming Body and Soul: Therapeutic Wisdom in the Gospel Stories.* New York/Mahwah, N.J.: Paulist Press, 1990.

Gould, Roger L. *Transformations: Growth and Change in Adult Life.* New York: Simon & Schuster, 1978.

Gross, Andrea. *Shifting Gears: Planning a New Strategy for Midlife.* New York: Crown, 1991.

Guntzelman, Joan. *Blessed Grieving.* Winona, Minn.: St. Mary's Press, 1985.

Halifax, Joan. *The Fruitful Darkness: Reconnecting with the Body of the Earth.* San Francisco: HarperSanFrancisco, 1993.

Hall, Nor. *The Moon and the Virgin: Reflections on the Archetypal Feminine.* New York: Harper & Row, 1980.

Hardin, Paula P. *What Are You Doing with the Rest of Your Life? Choices in Midlife.* San Rafael, Calif.: New World Library, 1992.

Harris, Maria. *Jubilee Time: Celebrating Women, Spirit, and the Advent of Age.* New York: Bantam, 1995.

Hillesum, Etty. *An Interrupted Life.* New York: Washington Square Press, 1985.

Hopkins, Patricia, and Sherry Ruth Anderson. *The Feminine Face of God: The Unfolding of the Sacred in Women.* New York: Bantam Books, 1991.

Houston, Jean. *The Search for the Beloved: Journeys in Sacred Psychology.* Los Angeles: Jeremy P. Tarcher, 1987.

Hover, Margot. *Women in the Middle: Facing Midlife Challenges with Faith.* Mystic, Conn.: Twenty-Third, 1995.

Hudson, Frederic M. *The Adult Years: Mastering the Art of Self-renewal.* San Francisco: Jossey-Bass, 1991.

Ingerman, Sandra. *Soul Retrieval.* San Francisco: HarperSanFrancisco, 1991.

Judy, Dwight H. *Healing the Male Soul: Christianity and the Mythic Journey.* New York: Crossroad, 1992.

Johnson, Elizabeth A. *Consider Jesus: Waves of Renewal in Christology.* New York: Crossroad, 1990.

Jung, Emma. *Animus and Anima.* Dallas: Spring, 1957.

Katchadourian, Henri. *Fifty — Midlife in Perspective.* New York: W. H. Freeman & Co., 1987.

Kaye, Elizabeth. *Mid-life: Notes from the Halfway Mark.* Reading, Mass.: Addison-Wesley, 1995.

Keck, Robert L. *Sacred Eyes.* Indianapolis: Knowledge Systems, 1992.

Keen, Sam. *Beginnings without End.* New York: Harper & Row, 1975.

Kidd, Sue Monk. *When the Heart Waits: Spiritual Direction for Life's Sacred Questions.* San Francisco: Harper & Row, 1990.

Kornfield, Jack. *A Path with Heart: A Guide through the Perils and Promises of Spiritual Life.* New York: Bantam Books, 1993.

Kubelka, Stanley. *Over Forty at Last: How to Ignore the "Mid-life Crisis" and Make the Most out of the Best Years of Your Life.* New York: Macmillan, 1980.

Kurtz, Jane. *Fire on the Mountain.* New York: Simon & Schuster, 1994.

Leech, Kenneth. *True Prayer: An Introduction to Christian Spirituality.* London: Sheldon Press, 1980.

Lehrman, Eric M. "The Psychospiritual Moratorium: An Investigation of the Dynamics of Psychospiritual Growth in Mid-life." Diss., Institute of Transpersonal Psychology, Palo Alto Calif., 1992.

L'Engle, Madeleine. *A Wind in the Door.* New York: Farrar, Straus & Giroux, 1973.

Leonard, Linda. *Witness to the Fire.* Boston: Shambhala, 1990.

Levine, Stephen. *Healing into Life and Death.* New York: Doubleday, 1987.

Levinson, Daniel J. *The Seasons of a Man's Life.* New York: Alfred A. Knopf, 1978.

Matthews, Caitlin. *Sophia Goddess of Wisdom: The Divine Feminine from Black Goddess to World Soul.* London: HarperCollins, 1991.

Merton, Thomas. *New Seeds of Contemplation.* New York: New Directions, 1961.

Mitchell, Kenneth, and Herbert Anderson. *All Our Losses All Our Griefs.* Philadelphia: Westminster Press, 1983.

Moore, Robert, and Douglas Gillette. *King, Warrior, Magician, Lover: Rediscovering the Archetype of the Mature Masculine.* San Francisco: HarperCollins, 1990.

Moore, Thomas. *Care of the Soul: A Guide for Cultivating Depth and Sacredness in Everyday Life.* New York: HarperCollins, 1992.

Murdock, Maureen. *The Heroine's Journey.* Boston and Shaftesbury: Shambhala, 1990.

Moustakas, Clark E. *Loneliness.* Englewood Cliffs, N.J.: Prentice-Hall, 1961.

Nichols, Michael P. *Turning Forty in the Eighties: Personal Crisis, Time for Change.* New York: W. W. Norton, 1986.

Noble, Kathleen. *The Sound of a Silver Horn: Reclaiming the Heroism in Contemporary Women's Lives.* New York: Fawcett Columbine, 1994.

Norris, Kathleen. *Dakota: A Spirituality of the Land.* New York: Tichnor & Fields, 1993.

Northrup, Christiane. *Women's Bodies, Women's Wisdom.* New York: Bantam Books, 1994.

Norwich, Julian. *Revelations of Divine Love.* Trans. M. L. del Mastro. New York: Doubleday, 1977.

O'Connor, Flannery. *The Habit of Being.* Ed. Sally Fitzgerald. New York: Farrar, Straus & Giroux, 1979.

O'Connor, Peter. *Understanding the Mid-life Crisis.* New York/Mahwah, N.J.: Paulist, 1981.

Oliver, Mary. *Selected Poems of Mary Oliver.* Boston: Beacon Press, 1992.

Orenstein, Gloria Feman. *Multi-cultural Celebrations: The Paintings of Betty LaDuke, 1972–1992.* San Francisco: Pomegranate Art Books, 1993.

Paladin, Lynda S. *Ceremonies for Change: Creating Rituals to Heal Life's Hurts.* Walpole, N.H.: Stillpoint, 1991.

Perera, Sylvia Brinton. *Descent to the Goddess.* Toronto: Inner City Books, 1981.

Powers, Jessica. *The House at Rest.* Carmelite Monastery, Meadowbrook Rd. Pewaukee, WI 53072, 1984.

Rountree, Cathleen. *On Women Turning Fifty: Celebrating Mid-Life Discoveries.* San Francisco: HarperSanFrancisco, 1993.

Rilke, Maria. *Letters to a Young Poet.* Trans. Herter Norton. New York: W. W. Norton, 1962.

Rubin, Lillian. *Women of a Certain Age: The Midlife Search for Self.* New York: Harper & Row, 1979.

Rupp, Joyce. *Praying Our Goodbyes.* Notre Dame, Ind.: Ave Maria Press, 1988.

———. *The Star in My Heart: Experiencing Sophia, Inner Wisdom.* San Diego: LuraMedia, 1990.

———. *Little Pieces of Light.* New York/Mahwah, N.J.: Paulist Press, 1994.

Sarton, May. *Plant Dreaming Deep.* New York: W. W. Norton, 1968.

———. *Journal of a Solitude*. New York: W. W. Norton, 1973.

Shannon William. *Thomas Merton's Dark Path*. New York: Farrar, Straus & Giroux, 1981.

Shaughnessy, Susan. *Walking on Alligators: A Book of Meditations for Writers*. San Francisco: HarperSanFrancisco, 1993.

Sheehy, Gail. *The Silent Passage — Menopause*. New York: Random House, 1991.

Siegel, Bernie. *Love, Medicine and Miracles: Lessons Learned about Self-healing from a Surgeon's Experience with Exceptional Patients*. New York: Harper & Row, 1986.

Siegfried, Regina, and Robert Morneau, eds. *Selected Poetry of Jessica Powers*, Kansas City: Sheed & Ward, 1989.

Singer, June. *The Gnostic Book of Hours*. San Francisco: HarperSanFrancisco, 1992.

Sleevi, MaryLou. *Sisters and Prophets*. Notre Dame, Ind.: Ave Maria Press, 1993.

Starck, Marcia, and Stern, Gynne. *The Dark Goddess*. Freedom, Calif.: Crossing Press, 1993.

Stein, Murray. *In Midlife*. Dallas: Spring, 1983.

Styron, William. *Darkness Visible: A Memoir of Madness*. New York: Random House, 1990.

Studzinski, Raymoud. *Spiritual Direction and Midlife Development*. Chicago: Loyola University Press, 1985.

Tagore, Rabindranath. *The Gitanjali*. New York: Macmillan, 1971.

Teilhard de Chardin, Pierre. *The Divine Milieu*. New York: Harper & Row, 1957.

Underhill, Evelyn. *The Ways of the Spirit*. Ed. Grace Adolphsen Brame. New York: Crossroad, 1990.

Ulanov, Ann Bedford. *The Wizard's Gate*. Einsiedeln, Switzerland: Daimon Verlag, 1994.

van der Post, Laurens. *A Mantis Carol*. Covelo, Calif.: Island Press, 1975.

Walker, Barbara. *The Crone: Wisdom, Age, Power*. New York: Harper & Row, 1985.

Wiederkehr, Macrina. *Seasons of Your Heart*. San Francisco: HarperSanFrancisco, 1991.

Wolkstein, Diane, and Noah S. Kramer. *Inanna, Queen of Heaven and Earth: Her Stories and Hymns from Sumner*. London: Rider Press, 1983.

Woodman, Marion. *The Pregnant Virgin: A Process of Psychological Transformation*. Toronto: Inner City Books, 1985.